Loss ↗
- Dignity at work
- p.6 key questions of book
- Balancing wk–fam. due to
  pressures at work
- p22 3 pillars of dignity at work
- Ees tied to bad jobs historically
  due to $
- ↑ in hours devoted to work

"As an economist, Paula Rayman brings an important and unique perspective to the most fundamentally important issue of our day 'having work that provides dignity and a family life that provides unrushed time for caring.' Rayman argues persuasively that externalities must be included in calculating the costs and benefits of our current economy. This new economic equation needs to consider what is productive for our economy, for the well-being of families, and for the viability of society. Rayman's views challenge current skepticism and cynicism, arguing that change in how we live and work is not only possible, but there are concrete signs it is beginning to occur."

—Ellen Galinsky, President, Families and Work Institute,
and author of *Ask the Children: The Breakthrough Study That
Reveals How To Succeed At Work And At Parenting*

"In searing portraits of America, its businesses, families, and its workers, Paula Rayman weaves together economics and sociology with a profound understanding of the quest for spiritual values in contemporary life. The book should serve as both an alarm bell and a guide book for politicians, CEOs, religious thinkers, the American worker—and for all those who recognize that America's future depends on restoring dignity, social responsibility, and balance to our work lives."

—Rabbi David Saperstein, Director,
Religious Action Center of Reform Judaism

BEYOND

the

BOTTOM LINE

The Search for Dignity at Work

Paula M. Rayman

palgrave

for St. Martin's Press

First published 2001 by
PALGRAVE™
175 Fifth Avenue, New York, N.Y.10010.
Companies and representatives throughout the world.

PALGRAVE is the new global publishing imprint of St. Martin's
Press LLC Scholarly and Reference Division and Palgrave Publishers Ltd (formerly Macmillan Press Ltd).

ISBN 0-312-22282-3 hardback

Library of Congress Cataloging-in-Publication Data
Rayman, Paula M.
    Beyond the bottom line : the search for dignity at work /
Paula M. Rayman
        p. cm.
    Includes bibliographical references and index.
    ISBN 0-312-22282-3
Work ethic. 2. Work--Psychological aspects. 3. Dignity. I.
Title.
    HD4905 .R35 2001
    158.7--dc21   00-046876

Design by Acme Art, Inc.

First edition: March 2001
10 9 8 7 6 5 4 3 2 1

Printed in the United States of America.

In honor of the life work of Rita R. Rayman

*In celebration of the future life work of
Alyssa and Lily Rayman-Read*

In appreciation of Rob Read's dignity in life and work

CONTENTS

ACKNOWLEDGEMENTS

This book was conceived over two decades ago, and its birth, after a very extended pregnancy, is due to many helpful hands. Foremost are the hundreds of people from near and afar who have shared their stories of work, family and community with me. These men and women have inspired my belief that the human search for dignity can be successful.

There are two other groups that deserve special recognition. First, my "readers" group, Sharon Bauer, Lisa Dodson, and Roz Feldberg, who acted as super midwives all through the process. Sharon reminded me that the turtle wins the race; Lisa urged me to keep my own voice; and Roz never let me forget how economic justice and dignity are interwoven. Second, my *havurah* group— Sharon and David, Judy and Peter—who have kept alive the spirit of nonviolence which taught me to keep my eyes on the prize.

A number of wonderful institutions over the years provided the space and sustenance for creative activity. Kibbutz Hanita offered a glimpse of how work could be organized to sustain family life. Boston College offered a congenial place to learn about conducting research across disciplinary boundaries. My Wellesley College and Bunting Institute experiences brought home the meaning of work in the lives of women of all ages from all walks of life. And most recently, Radcliffe College and now Radcliffe Institute of Advanced Study at Harvard University made resources of time, space, and research assistance generously available. President Linda Wilson graciously provided professional leave time, and Acting Dean Mary Dunn was a source of optimism and levity in the midst of institutional change.

The National Institute of Mental Health, the Alfred P. Sloan Foundation, and the Ford Foundation have given financial resources for different research efforts I have undertaken over the years on work, family, and community. I am grateful for their support.

Many colleagues at Radcliffe and Harvard and from other settings shared ideas, suggestions, and insights from their own research and activities. I would like to thank especially Ann Bookman, Susan Eaton, David Ellwood, Netsy Firestein, Richard Freeman, Mitchell Fromstein, Marshall Gans, David Hamburg, Renee Landers, Katherine Newman, Jane Mansbridge, Martha Minow, Robert Reich and the Finletter pizza group, Juliet Schor, Robert Solow, Mette Sorenson, Anne Szostak, Robert Weiss, Marina Whitman, and Lyn Williams. James Carroll was the guide who led me to begin with Genesis and then to Pope Leo; Robert Parker provided leads to Protestant teachings, and Rabbi Everett Gendler and Rabbi Daniel Gropper gave guidance about Judaic texts on creation and work. Wally and Juanita Nelson, in their steadfast upholding of nonviolence, reminded me of the strength of the humanist tradition and the import of "doing no harm."

The book would have never seen the light of day without the incredible support of colleagues at the Radcliffe Public Policy Center. Leslie Cintron, research analyst, has been remarkable with her ability to track down data and make it useful! During the last three years, student research partners have done invaluable work, acting as detectives to leave no stone unturned. My deepest thanks to Chiwen Bao, Corrine Calfee, Patricia Fessler, Kristin Gore, Kirstin Hill, Vedica Jain, Michelle Lee, Veronica Lopez, Priscilla Merriam, Ozge Saritosun, Kristi Schaeffer, Jasmin Sethi, and Julie Stewart.

Fellows and staff at PPC have helped create an environment of work that has allowed me to "walk the talk" of integrating work and family and community. Matina Horner Visiting Professors Lotte

Bailyn, Martha Chen, Marian Ferber, and Deborah Stone have enriched my understanding of work and life. Fellows Fauzia Ahmad, Robert Kuttner, Gail Leftwich, Ruchama Marton, Pamela Stone, and Sharland Trotter from their diverse fields of knowledge and passionate commitment to their work shared wisdom and encouragement. No one could ask for a better staff of team players than Angela Place, Sue Shefte, Françoise Carré, Abby Elmore, Nancy Waters, Tiffany Manuel, and Shannon Quinn. And special thanks to Kris Locke for her continual support on both the work and family fronts.

From my first meeting with Karen Wolny of Palgrave I knew I had found an editor who shared a vision for the book project. Her thorough and thoughtful readings of many drafts and firm but gentle pushes to go beyond my initial stopping places made a great difference to what is valuable in this book. I would also like to thank Alan Bradshaw, Meredith Howard, Amy McDermott, Robert Oppedisano, Gabriella Pearce, Jennifer Reeve, Peter Rooney, Roberta Scheer, Harriet Seltzer, and Dori Weintraub for their respective labors in bringing this book to fruition.

And my appreciation to my family is boundless. My mother has always encouraged me to work to make the world a better place and to keep trying despite hard times. Lily never let me forget that in the past I often failed to live up to what I preached but has admitted I am improving, and Alyssa has asked penetrating questions from her generation of women to mine. My husband, Rob, continues to be my haven from the heartless world, and his quiet dignity is a steady beacon of hope.

PREFACE

In 1958 my father lost his work. He did not lose a "job," because he was a self-employed businessman who never wanted to work for someone else. He came to America in 1912 to escape the pogroms on the Polish-Russian border, where his family of 11 siblings and parents had eked out a living from a small dishes and pottery store. Soon after his arrival, he enlisted in the U.S. Army. During World War I, as quartermaster sergeant, he managed to send some supplies to his family overseas and save enough to enroll in school at the Cooper Union in New York City when the war was over. From then on he began one small business after another, from drug stores to dry cleaning operations, finally settling on a two-man import-export firm in the 1940s that traded in a remarkable array of goods: rugs from Rumania, watches from Switzerland, bananas and beef from South and Central America.

Wherever he went, my father learned the native tongue, so by the time he married at the end of World War II, he could converse in half a dozen languages. Soon after I was born in 1947, the once proud bachelor named an imported Danish ham after me, complete with a picture of a dark-haired girl on the label. This always struck me as a mixed message since my mother kept a strictly kosher home, and I would have preferred a more exotic product to bear my name.

For a few years after the war, my father did well, and we lived in a nice hotel flat on Manhattan's upper West Side. But after my sister's birth in the 1950s, the bottom fell out of my father's business. There was a tremendous shift in the American economy after World

War II, as we moved into a world of multinational corporations and the market expansion of a global economy. In the 1950s many small businesses lost their footing, resulting in the demise of many small firms. But at the time we did not understand that my father's loss fit into some larger trend. Around us, families, often cashing in on the GI Bill, were buying new homes in the suburbs, commuting in newly purchased cars, and going to college in record numbers. America seemed alive, growing, and full of hope.

In our house I remember my father, who had been a gregarious, generous man who liked to be the life of a party, becoming more and more withdrawn, unable to find work because nobody wanted to hire a man over 60 who had never worked for anyone. My mother, who had had polio as a child, went from home to home teaching physically disabled children, earning barely enough to keep a roof over our heads. The costs to our family from my father's unemployment were financial and emotional. My father hated no longer being the breadwinner and was filled with shame and anger that my mother was the primary provider. The house filled with a sense of constant, unspoken worry. My mother and I, in an act of mortification amidst our wealthier neighbors, went door to door selling eggs to gain extra needed dollars.

Finally, my father found a low-paying job in a packing warehouse, but his cigarette-ravaged lungs wore out, and he died a slow, cruel death from emphysema and lung cancer. In one of his last letters to me as I started college, he said, "When I am better, I hope to be back at work again!" For my father, having work was essential to his dignity. There was no worthwhile life without work.

❖ ❖ ❖

Thus, the roots of this book are grounded in the hard-learned lessons from my early childhood. In the 1970s, I spent years searching for where "good work" existed: in utopian tracts and novels; in a year on an Israeli kibbutz that embraced the notion "from each according to their ability, to each according to their need"; in women's groups trying to figure out the relationship of paid work, family commitments, and success.

In my own job search, I sought out an occupation that would offer a decent livelihood, a chance to balance work and family, and an opportunity to contribute to the larger society. Teaching had worked this way for my mother, and I followed in her path, though at the university rather than the elementary level. My first teaching courses, responding to the increasing violence in American society, turned to the theory and practice of nonviolence. And the nonviolent movements of the world offered persuasive examples of work with dignity.

Gandhi, in his quest for India's freedom from colonialism, had linked the concept of *sarovadaya,* or uplifting of all, to national liberation. He grasped that good work builds self-esteem in the individual while connecting each person to the larger community. All over India, the spinning wheel became the symbol of national freedom. The spinning wheel gave the people of India constructive work, livelihood, and a means to national self-sufficiency—if you could spin your own cloth, you no longer had to be dependent on imported wares. Men, women, and children learned skills and produced what they wore, weaving together by the hundreds in community squares. Out of their work together came a sense of national solidarity despite regional differences.

In contrast, in the United States work has been defined in individual terms: a person is individually responsible for success or failure at work. A vivid way to discover the meaning of work in America is to listen to the voices of those who have lost jobs—from the depression years of the 1930s to the more recent events of downsizing and reengineering in the 1990s. For years, my research reflected interviews I conducted with people across America who had lost their work. They showed me how terrible the costs were in personal and social terms. In the United States the costs are especially painful because the victims of job loss blame themselves. Even if the entire plant shuts down, even if you are one of the 14,000 ATT workers laid off in one devastating year, the power of shame is overwhelming. If you believe the American Horatio Alger credo of pulling oneself up the ladder and then you fall off, it must be because you misstepped.

❖ ❖ ❖

The American overemphasis on autonomy undermines the achievement of dignity in the workplace. Dignity rests on both independence and interdependence, a reality that economist and Nobel Prize laureate Amartya Sen terms "the interdependences of social living."[1] Dignity refers to the intrinsic worth of each human being, and the realization of dignity is either enhanced or reduced by how human beings treat one another.[2] In the human struggle for achieving dignity, each of us strives within the contexts in which we live—within our institutions of family, work, and community. And since work experience is so much, so deep a part of each of our lives, whether our work situation affirms our dignity—indeed, whether we are able to work at all—shapes our freedom to realize dignity.

At a recent gathering of women leaders in York, Maine, Martin Luther King's famous "Letter from a Birmingham Jail" was the focus of a discussion of the moral issues in economic development. His powerful language provided a compelling moral argument for the civil rights movement and its connection to basic political and economic rights. Condemning a culture that labels a six-year-old child inferior because she is black, King speaks of the need for all human beings to fight for human dignity so no person faces a degenerating sense of "nobodiness."[3]

It was this nobodiness that my father experienced when he lost his work. In our culture having no work makes you a nobody, a person whose freedom to experience dignity is compromised and, in some cases, lost. For those of us who get up each day and go to work—in offices, in factories, in homes, and on farms, on airplanes or on computers—the dignity that rests on the "interdependences" of life at work is not easily gained.

❖ ❖ ❖

It is clear that slaves are not treated with dignity by their masters. But in the emerging global economy, with its fervid embrace of a bottom-line mentality, many employees and many workers are also reduced to instruments of econometric goals of efficiency. In human history large groups of people—slaves, serfs, and sweatshop laborers—were treated without respect for their humanity. The expectation in modern times has been that democratic principles and technological innovations will free us from tyranny. But the global economy poses a different form of oppression—an entrapment in a never-ending cycle of overwork, pressured consumption, and exhaustion from trying to get ahead and to find time. We wind up living in ways we would prefer to change but we feel we have no choice. Our lives seem less than they could be.

With all the wealth that surrounds us in America, many families still do not have adequate health care, housing, or education. Women, racial minorities, and those in low-skilled jobs still have not gotten their fair share of the wealth. And middle-class and professional employees—even with official titles and decent salaries—live rushed, frantic lives. As workers and as customers in the market economy, we are expendable, interchangeable, and there is no humanizing of our daily activities. The tyranny of the new economy is that as workers and as customers, no one really knows our name.

And thus, we are deprived of being treated with dignity—not as dramatically as slaves but on a slippery slope of devaluation. As legal scholar Fred Schauer explains, to reduce people to the status of a tool or instrument for the ambitions, the aspirations, or the goals of another "is the essence of what deprivation of dignity is all about."[4]

The interaction of confirming oneself through work and being confirmed by others is necessary for a person to attain a sense of dignity. This is equally true for women and men. Decades ago, research on paid work and unemployment ignored women, which reflected the prevailing view expressed in Freud's *Civilization and Its Discontents* that women's lives rested only on love. My interviews with women who have lost paid work and with women who feel devalued doing care-giving work document that the need for dignity at work for women is as real as it is for men.[5]

Producing opportunities for work with dignity for all citizens is also an essential function of a democratic society. The Greek term *idiot* was applied to persons who did not function as responsible social citizens. If we lose hope in the dignity of our workplaces and public institutions, we risk having a nation of idiots. As Gandhi understood, individual self-sufficiency and national independence are interdependent. If people do not feel they can attain dignity at work, they lose the trust and hope necessary to sustain the public institutions vital for democracy. Without the promise of work with dignity, the sparks for creativity, for teamwork, for investment in the future die.

❖ ❖ ❖

In 1998, 40 years after my father's unemployment, my college-age daughter asked me the question, "Can you work and have a life?"

For her, the pressing issue was not being without work but rather the desire for meaningful work that also allowed a quality life. As she and many young people look at the baby boomers and older cohorts, they see people running faster and faster to stay in place. Young women question if the legacy of the women's movement was only to press for women to fill men's shoes in the rat race scramble to the top. Young men increasingly wonder if they can break out of the breadwinner role pressures to "be a man." They want the freedom to take more time for care-giving roles for their families.

Everyone, young and old, today is desperately seeking dignity at work, which provides time and energy for a good life. In today's speeded-up economy, some of the most intractable threats to dignity arise from work being organized in ways that undermine family and care-giving time and time for civic participation. The costs we bear from such work arrangements and work demands are significant: they prevent us from being with the people we most care for in the ways they need and in the ways we need to be there for our own sense of well-being. Most of us do not have sufficient time to be with our children, to be with our aging parents, to be with our friends and loved ones, to have time for reflection and recreation. Skewed priorities that push people to work mandatory overtime and long 50- to 60-hour work weeks cause immense pressures on individuals and families. The way work is organized today has undermined the time-out period, the concept of sacred time, or the Sabbath that Adam and Eve and even God respected.

And, it prevents us from being engaged in socially responsible activities that are necessary to preserve the fabric of our society and our democratic institutions. The time and effort we need to protect our civil and political rights are vital not only to sustain our democratic way of life, but also to sustain economic well-being. So we need to invest time in our democratic way of life if we want in the future to reap the riches from a political, social, and economic harvest. But given our present work reality, which threatens our dignity on many levels, far too few of us can confidently assure that we and our children and our grandchildren will be able to reap that harvest.

❖ ❖ ❖

Can we achieve dignity at work in the emerging economy? That is the question that propels this book. In the last decades, books, talk shows, and chat rooms have promoted new formulas for success, for achieving excellence, for balancing work and family, and for becoming a more perfect self. But an underlying uneasiness continues for many of us as we attempt to fit the pieces of our lives together. Even in the midst of an economic boom time, something of value seems beyond our reach.

We are living in an age that undermines our freedom to achieve dignity. The way work is currently organized for most of us—as we will see through the real-life examples and case-studies of professionals, middle-income dual-income employees, semiskilled and unskilled workers—blocks us from our dignity. A global economy that promotes only a bottom-line mentality prevents our attainment of dignity. It is time to look beyond the bottom line. This is a wake-up call to explore the costs of doing business as usual—for ourselves, for our families, for our society.

SECTION

Roots

ONE

Genesis
Three Pillars of Dignity at Work

And, male and female He created them . . . On the
seventh day God finished the work that He had been
doing and He rested on the seventh day from all the
work that He had done . . . The Lord God took man
and placed him in the garden of Eden to till and tend
it. God created man in His image, in the image of God
He created them.

—Genesis

I feel like I go home, and basically I have dinner, go to
bed, and get up in the morning to go back to work. I
feel like I'm on a treadmill, becoming less and less each
day . . .

—computer technician, Los Angeles

MODERN LESSONS FROM ADAM AND EVE

In the beginning, Adam and Eve had a lot of work to do. They had the honest, blue-collar work of tillers of the soil. They could see the fruits of their hands as seeds grew to plants and provided food for sustenance. Maybe at first there were only two or three kinds of vegetables, and Adam preferred growing more tomatoes while Eve wanted endless rows of corn. But they compromised and worked hard together, continuing the process of creation and became coworkers. Through their work, they were able to sustain themselves, providing a livelihood.

They also took on the more white-collar occupation of naming things around them. This involved a lot of intense mental energy given the number of plants and animals abounding in nature. But they persevered and got the job done.

The combination of seeing the work of one's hands and gaining a sense of empowerment from naming the surrounding creatures gave both Adam and Eve a sense of achievement, a joy in a job well done. They could look at each other as they worked and see the other acknowledging the work done. So each felt the strong sense of self-respect that comes when you know you have done a job well.

All their work was also making a difference in the world. They could see that they were having an impact on the earth. It made them feel connected to the larger world around them. They understood that as they worked the soil, the soil gave back something. Their work was part of a larger process and gave each day's work a larger purpose. To be human meant being connected not only to your loved ones but to the larger world as well.

So, through their work Adam and Eve gained a livelihood, self-respect, and connection to the larger world. There was dignity in their work, in their existence. These three pillars of dignity at work—livelihood, self-respect, and social responsibility—set the foundation for all the future generations.

Sustaining dignity was not easy. Adam and Eve were part of a family. Eve was definitely the one who gave birth to the original next generation, first to Cain and then to Abel. This was probably the most dangerous and strenuous labor undertaken so far by a human being. But afterward, how did they manage the work-family issue? Did he till while she breast-fed? Did they both wake at night to rock the cradle? Who made sure the boys did not wander into danger? The struggle for work, family, and gender roles had begun. How could the work that needed to be done be organized so that it enhanced rather than undermined family life?

Adam and Eve tried to balance the tilling and naming jobs with raising the boys. Sometimes they were running harder and harder just to stay in place. The need for sacred time, a time for renewal and reflection, was deeply felt. Even the Spirit of the Universe did not work 24/7 and had rested after the six days of creation. In addition to creating all the things in space, it was essential to create a special moment in time. Without the reality of a Sabbath, there would be endless days of labor, with no time to appreciate the fruits of the labor. Dignity at work depended on taking time for R and R.

The boys grew up and, just as their parents', their lives provide lessons for our own work-life struggles. Their story sheds light on the first human encounters with reengineering and unemployment.

When Cain and Abel grew into manhood, the first clear case of division of labor occurred. Cain followed in his parents' footsteps as a tiller of the soil, but Abel stepped out to become a keeper of the sheep. The brothers' tale, also demonstrating an early case of sibling rivalry, has the tiller killing the shepherd. On learning of Cain's murder of Abel, God banishes the tiller from the soil, saying the soil will no longer "yield its strength to you." Cain protests that the banishment from his work as "too great a punishment." He cannot imagine that he can endure a life without his work as a tiller. His skills are not easily transferable, and there are no adult education classes to attend. Cain loses his roots, his livelihood, his dignity. He is forced to be an aimless wanderer upon the earth.

Adam and Eve and their children present us with the questions that are threaded through human history and that propel this book: Whether we are in the garden of Eden or thrust into the desert, whether we are in a period of economic boom or bust, can we find the three pillars that sustain dignity at work—livelihood, self-respect, and social responsibility? In our new global economy, as changing technology allows us to save time but also makes us run faster and faster to stay in place, can we and our children have work and a life? In an expanding market economy that reveres a bottom-line mentality, do we attain economic success only at the dangerous cost of losing our human dignity?

PRESENT PARABLES

We now fast-forward from Adam and Eve to about 5,000 years later.

In the year 2000, Kate is a 40-year-old lawyer who realizes that she is definitely not in the garden of Eden.[1] When she started law school in the 1980s, she was one of thousands of women who were entering the professional gates of law and medicine in record numbers, turning their backs on the more traditional occupations for females of nursing, clerical jobs, and teaching. She thought she could do it all—the supermom who had a great and challenging career, an ambitious but supportive partner, and a loving set of children. In the year 2000, she knows she cannot be a supermom, and she knows she does not *want* to be a supermom.

When I interviewed Kate, she had just made a life-changing decision: she was going to end her full-time position and quest to become a law partner and instead be a part-time staff attorney. The grind of working in a law firm, where the normal work week averages 60 to 70 hours, where the people who have prestige are those who have the most billable hours regardless of their inefficiency, where there is little time for parenting and care giving, had taken its toll.

In Kate's words, "I was told to be valuable, and to the firm, this meant racking up at least 50 billed hours per week, 50 weeks a year. That is 2,500 hours. Some people in my firm were claiming over 3,000 hours. My biological clock was running out, and I finally had a partner, and I wanted to spend time [with him] without feeling so out of it that I had nothing to give anyone. I was running around trying to find time, and there was no time."

Kate was hitting the billable-hour burnout. Billable hours are essentially the hours that firms charge to clients and did not actually become widely used in the legal profession until the 1960s. The advent of new technology in the sixties made the concept of hourly billing not only possible but desirable. The use of automated accounting systems, beginning in the 1950s and enhanced by computers thereafter, allowed efficient recording and allocation of an attorney's time. Just as the invention of the clock revolutionized the workplace in the 1500s, the computer transformed how Kate's work could be measured. And in our economy, we measure what we value.

Billable hours became a powerful tool to record and measure Kate's effort, and each inputted hour of her work was assigned a dollar value. Her value to the firm was thought of in terms of how many billable hours she had, not unlike the auto industry valuing its blue-collar labor by how many cars per hour roll off the assembly line.

But Kate trained for years to be a professional, not a blue-collar line worker. Indeed, her income—over $175,000—was enough to earn her a label as a highly successful woman at work. Yet, Kate felt something was wrong. "The whole thing rewards you for working ineffectively—the longer a product takes you to get done for a client, the more hours you can bill. The better for the firm, the worse for the client. No one cares about the quality of my work. I started feeling like a fraud. I was so committed to being a good lawyer, someone doing well for my clients, and now I had to choose between being someone valuable to my firm or being true to my professional training."

So Kate is going to start to work part-time, which for her means 35 to 40 hours a week (a full-time job in most places!). And the new road she has chosen is not all roses. As Cynthia Fuchs Epstein, a noted sociologist who studied part-time legal jobs, reports, "Individuals who work what most people would regard as a normal work week but less than the workaholic time standard of their firm [are] stigmatized in both trivial and profound ways."[2] Kate faces managers who may refuse to give her a title appropriate to her seniority, who will schedule meetings at times she cannot make, who will punish her with loss of status for not putting in enough "face time" if she is not there late in the day or on weekends.

But she wants to start a family, and she wants to have a life. Kate has begun to craft a solution by taking more control of her time. She wishes her law firm was more "family friendly," more creative in how work could get done. But, alone, she cannot change the entire corporate culture. So Kate is taking charge of what she can do. She is in search of dignity at work.

❖   ❖   ❖

Dan, 34, is a few years younger than Kate and the father of two children, ages four and six. He is a corporate controller at a small biotech firm, where he has worked for the last five years. His wife works full-time—over 50 hours a week—which matches his weekly toll. Two years ago, they bought their first home near where they grew up and her parents still live. The location of their home purchase was strategic because they rely heavily upon their relatives for helping to care for the kids. In fact, Dan, like increasing numbers of young employees, refused to move to another location to begin a higher-paying job due to family reasons.[3]

After four years of college, Dan did staff-level accounting for one of the big banks in Boston in 1986, at a starting salary of $19,000 per year. By 1990, he had advanced to assistant controller and was making $26,000, but as he was about to get married, he realized that he was not much of a breadwinner. With the costs of housing, heating, and health care rocketing sky-high in Massachusetts, he knew he needed to make more to have a decent shot at getting his share of the American dream. So in 1993 he made an industry change. "I decided to go into an industry that looked good for growth and for income, so I switched to biotech."

There are a lot of things Dan likes about the biotech industry. "I have the chance to develop my own abilities. I like the products we are working on, which makes me feel like I am accomplishing something for myself and for others." When questioned, Dan agreed that even if he did not need the money, he would continue to work. In 1999 Dan's salary was up to $71,000, his firm and Dan benefiting from the booming economy and the success of clinical trials for the new state-of-the-art drugs coming from their efforts.

So Dan has a good livelihood, he has self-respect that comes from using and developing his skills, and he feels the work he is doing contributes to the well-being of the larger society. His grasp on dignity at work seems secure. But when I asked him about his sense of security and the future, his grasp seemed less sure. "My wife and I are working really hard, and often work hits up against family, and sometimes family hits up against work. If the folks weren't there, we couldn't survive. And they are getting older, and then they will need care, and I don't know what we'll do. I am worried about my future and for my family's security."

Even in the midst of plenty, Dan suggests he is not secure. And interestingly, when asked if he would be proud if his children went into his line of work, he responded with a firm "No!" Surprised by the strength of his reaction, I asked him why. "Because, in my firm if you are not a senior scientist, you do not get all the respect you deserve." It turns out that Dan feels that his colleagues do not recognize his contributions to the firm's success—that in some ways, his work is more invisible than theirs. Thus, his sense of self-respect is diminished when he sees himself through their eyes. He knows he is doing a good job, but he wants more. He wants them to acknowledge his worth. Self-respect, a key piece of dignity, seems an interactive process, coming from within and without. On the spectrum of the dignity continuum, Dan almost has it all. But not completely.

❖　❖　❖

Joan is a 52-year-old home health care worker, who spent her first working years sending paychecks to her family in the Caribbean and, more recently, acted as a single parent to her ill sister's three teenage children. After finishing high school, she did a string of low-paying jobs: waitressing, working in a fish-packing factory, a clerical job processing paperwork for the financial sector. She never made more than $6.50 an hour. Through a friend's urging, she took a certificate course to become a dietary aide and then moved into home health care. Like most home health care aides in America, Joan is a low-paid female worker. Nearly 90 percent of nurses and personal care workers are women, and many—one out of three—are minority women. Since 1998, Joan has primarily been working with elderly residents of a senior citizens complex, going from unit to unit to help people get out of bed, wash, dress, and feed themselves.

Working for an agency, she strives to meet the goals put forth by the organization and at the same time meet the needs for those who rely on her for care. In her words, "I love my work, helping out people, so they're feeling better about themselves. But there is always so much to get done, and I have to move on to get to the next person, even if the person I'm with still needs something."

So much of the care giving in our nation has shifted from nonpaid informal care to what Deborah Stone calls "public care"— care giving by professionals and paraprofessionals through profit and nonprofit firms, all regulated to some degree by government agencies.[4] And Joan, like the home health care workers Stone studied, constantly feels she has to break the rules that her employer sets in order to provide good care. Joan illustrated her dilemma by describing an incident that happened a week before. "I just finished getting Mrs. Smith from her bath and got her all dressed, when she asked me to help her get some boxes down that she could not reach. Her closet was a real mess, and I knew it would take me some time to do this for her. I wanted to help her, but I am only supposed to take care of certain health things for her. And I was running late to get to my next person. But there was no one else to help, so there I was doing the boxes."

Joan's next thought revealed how she gets dignity in her work. "When I finished the boxes, the biggest smile was on Mrs. Smith's face, she said I was the best! It was worth it even if it was not supposed to happen." Joan resolves the dilemma through her determination to "to do the right thing," even if it is outside the rules of her employing agency. This is how she keeps her sense of dignity.

Joan says she comes home dead tired each day, and she often has paperwork she needs to finish up as she tries to make sure the kids get their homework done. Yet, she thinks she is "doing better now than ever before," having an income she can count on that pays the bills, a job where she feels she is "doing good," and a feeling of pride that she does "skillful work."

So Joan right now would say she has work with dignity, even if the way she does her job—putting emphasis on the caring relationship of her work—collides with the goals of her employer, which emphasize productivity in terms of how many people are seen per day by each worker and limiting the number of days people are eligible for care. She has dignity at her work despite her employer.

Joan knows there are real costs to real people if she does not do her job her way. Her fear is that physically she may not be able to keep this up and that she could lose her health coverage. She has no pension plan through her work and little savings. For Joan, having good health care coverage and a pension, even better a "portable pension" to cover her job changes, would move her closer to having work with dignity. She wonders who will take care of her when she gets to be the age of "her people." If there is no one there, will she be able to keep up her dignity?

❖ ❖ ❖

And then there are the workers who are so on the margins of our economy that they rarely appear on our vision screen: the farm workers who toil so we get our fruits and vegetables, the poultry workers who skin and gut our chickens, the environment workers at the material recovery facilities who clean up our garbage, and the over one-half million domestic workers counted by the Census Bureau (the majority of whom are not counted since the servant economy is still mostly underground). These people are seen, in Barbara Ehrenreich's words, as "lower kinds of people for a lower kind of work."[5]

In the early 1980s, an African American graduate student, Judith Rollins, whose dissertation I was supervising, did a study of domestic service by becoming a household servant herself. Although a highly intelligent person, she found herself seen as a "lower kind" of person, rendered invisible by her white female employers, who would talk to their spouses as if she were not there in the same room and offer her used clothing even though she was neatly dressed. They did not see her. Her book *Between Women* became a classic accounting of how race, class, and gender intersect to shape the interaction of employer and employee. When she shared her experience, she said she was deeply affected by how hard it was to keep dignity in the face of "being a nobody." Not only her mind had been discounted but her very bodily existence.

Newspapers in June 2000 reported that 60 Chinese workers, seeking a better livelihood and a chance to become part of the "haves" of our booming economy, suffocated to death in a truck supposedly carrying them to freedom. The illegal workers were packed into the truck's container and sealed in with the air vent closed as the heat soared. The workers struggled in vain to pry open the vents and banged frantically on the walls with their shoes to get attention that did not arrive until too late. Here the most poor and desperate workers were treated as if they were beyond the human dignity spectrum. These Chinese workers, just as women trafficked across borders in a human slave-prostitution trade, just as barely surviving informal sector workers the world over, were not granted eligibility for the basic human rights of livelihood, respect, and membership in the human community.

❖ ❖ ❖

In our times, we have unequal access to dignity at work and we fall at various points along the dignity spectrum. Kate and Joan and Dan and Judith represent many of us in America. From Kate and Joan, we see that bottom-line goals of more billable hours and more clients per day erode the quality of work they can perform. Dan, with a good job in a growth industry, continues to be worried about security for himself and his family. Judith was an invisible worker, viewed as a nobody, whose sense of dignity must have come from within if it was to exist. And in a global economy suffused with a bottom-line mentality, much of the world's labor force—marginal, in the informal sector, and often female—are left out of the economic boom and left off the dignity spectrum.[6]

The threats to dignity at work are different depending on where we stand in the economic scheme of things, our race, our gender, our class, as well as other defining categories shaping our experiences. The erosion of accessibility to dignity seems paradoxical in a time of plenty and in a period of amazing technological advances.

Under the new rules of the global economy can we attain economic prosperity only at the cost of losing dignity at work? Economist Marina Whitman in *New World, New Rules* proposes that there may be stark trade-offs between the risk and fluidity necessary to sustain economic growth and the resultant increase in economic inequality and insecurity. Free market globalists and human rights internationalists seem on a collision course as the twenty-first century begins. Perhaps only an elite can expect to work and have a life while the majority are sent out like Cain to be wanderers in a world of insecurity, continual stress, and diminishing expectations.

Issues of economic security, work-life balance, growing inequality, and finding time for a meaningful existence are in the hearts and minds of Americans across our nation. We, as a people and as a nation, are searching for daily meaning as well as daily bread. And we know in our souls that dignity is as significant to our existence as financial reward.

DIGNITY: A WORKING DEFINITION

There is no simple definition for dignity. The word dignity comes from the Latin word *dignitas*, meaning worth and merit, and *dignus*, meaning worthy. Webster's dictionary goes on to define dignity as "the quality of being worthy" and having "pride and self-respect."

The modern notion of dignity is grounded in the Enlightenment movement of the 1700s, which shifted access to dignity from an exclusive feature of the nobility to an inherent feature common to all human beings.[7]

Dignity has to do with the essence of who we are as human beings. It is an ultimate value that makes human life worthwhile. Historically, the philosopher most associated with discussion of the dignity of human beings is Immanuel Kant. His famous dictum formulates that dignity is priceless: "In the Kingdom of ends everything has either a price or a dignity. If it has a price, something else can be put in its place as an equivalent: if it is exalted above all price and so admits of no equivalent, then it has a dignity."[8] In contrasting dignity with price, Kant's view is that human beings have a dignity that transcends their particular social standing and is based on each person's capacity to make universal moral laws which then govern their lives. Unlike other commodities in life, dignity is beyond price and not for sale.

Dignity is something beyond the bottom line.

The origins of this natural dignity, according to Kant's contemporaries Thomas Paine and Mary Wollstonecraft, reside in the rights of all rational human beings. For these philosophers, human dignity resided in the capacity of human beings to be rational, which set them apart from other living creatures. And Wollstonecraft's emphasis on all human beings was a major step forward for gender equality.

For theologians, the origins of dignity and human rights in general reflect the belief that each human being is sacred, made in the image of God, and thus eligible to have dignity. Without God, according to religious doctrine, human beings would not have human rights and would not have dignity. Human beings exist only within the world of transcendent moral laws. They argue that the essence of being human, of experiencing human dignity, is that which brings us closest to being in the image of God.

For secularists, human beings are the measure of all things. To act with dignity means living up to your essential worth. Being treated with dignity means being treated in accord with your essential worth. Their defense of human dignity depends on the idea of moral reciprocity and the capacity of human beings to be empathetic. As Michael Ignatieff proposes, "The strength of a purely secular ethics is its insistence that there are no sacred purposes which can ever justify the inhuman use of human beings."[9]

From both of these perspectives, dignity is a dynamic process. For religious believers, dignity emanates from a human being's relationship with God: made in God's image, an individual experiences dignity by acting according to God's commandments and moral laws. For secularists, reciprocity of behavior between human beings is the key: we act toward another with a sense of dignity, so we ourselves are treated with dignity. Our sense of self is interdependent with other people in our lives, in our communities, and, if we can think large enough, with all others in our world.

DIGNITY AT WORK

Since so many of our life hours are spent at work, striving to achieve dignity in life, whether we hold to religious or secularist views, is inextricably connected to dignity at work. As noted, society plays its role in defining dignity at work by the way it confers value on our paid and unpaid jobs. This makes an enormous difference in our access to dignity or our "dignity freedom."[10]

The street sweeper in our society, no matter how well he sweeps, receives little appreciation and respect, and thus much of his dignity must be self-generated. Martin Luther King, Jr. once said, "If a man is called to be a street sweeper, he should sweep streets even as Michelangelo painted or Beethoven conducted music or Shakespeare wrote poetry. He should sweep streets so well that all the hosts of heaven and earth will pause to say, here lived a great street sweeper who did his job well."[11]

But acting as King suggested isn't easy. Many workers in such jobs, burdened with other deprivations in their lives, do not have a reservoir of internal dignity to draw upon when their dignity is continually assaulted by employers and others who devalue their efforts. In our market economy, parking lot attendants who care for cars make more, are valued more, than day care teachers who tend our children. Society, by placing value on different occupations and determining how work is organized, creates conditions that either enhance or detract from our ability to experience dignity.

In 1935, 25-year-old Simone Weil, the highly regarded French writer and social commentator, began work in an electrical machine factory on rue LeCourbe in Paris. Always tired, she lived in fear of not being able to meet the work quotas necessary to maintain her job. Her job entailed placing large copper bobbins pierced with holes in a furnace so the fire could pass through them and then taking them out a few moments later. A new worker, she did not know how to avoid the flames. During her first day on the job, when Simone was scorched while pulling out the bobbins, a fellow welder opposite her gave her an empathetic smile. It was moment of humanity amidst the humiliation.

In her *Factory Journal,* Simone summed up her initial experience: "The capital fact is not the suffering but the humiliation. The feeling of personal dignity as it has been formed by society is shattered." In a letter to her friend Albertine after a year of such work, she said, "Don't imagine that this provoked in me any rebellious action. No, on the contrary, it produced the last thing I expected from me—docility . . . It seemed to me that I was born to wait for, and receive, and carry out orders, that I had never done and never would do anything else. I am not proud of this confession."[12]

What does this diary of work begin to tell us about dignity? First, having dignity is experienced as being the opposite of experiencing humiliation or a lessening of the self. It also suggests that a clear understanding of dignity emerges when it is lost. This is not unlike the wise words of sociologist and ethnographer Egon Bitner: "If you wish to understand the meaning of work in society, study the consequences of unemployment."[13] It is often easier for us to know when someone has dissed us, to use a popular current phrase, than to be aware of when our dignity is intact.

DIGNITY AND WELL-BEING

The late AIDS researcher Dr. Jonathan Mann focused attention on the relationship between dignity and sustaining health. He developed an exercise to investigate dignity by focusing on its violation. Participants in the experiment were asked to recall a situation in which they felt their personal dignity had been violated. Mann found that dignity flowed from two interacting components: one internal (how I see myself) and the other external (how others see me). The dignity violations reported by the participants fell into four categories: not being seen; being seen but only as part of a group; loss of safe personal space; and humiliation, especially by being separated out for criticism in front of others.[14]

These four types of violations were discussed as real, everyday situations in the health care system. For example, when a physician refused to make eye contact with a patient, patients reported feeling disregarded and unheard in such situations. In a more extreme variation, there is evidence that guards in Nazi concentration camps were told never to look into the eyes of inmates. This assured that the human-ness of inmates would not be seen, thus creating a major violation of personal dignity.

Being seen only as a member of a group is a second category of dignity violation. An example in the health care system is a situation in which a woman suffering a heart attack is not treated as aggressively as a man would be because her symptoms are often dismissed as "women's complaints." Despite the seriousness of her condition, her voice goes unheard, the truthfulness of her concerns is denied, her dignity is attacked because she is grouped as being "one of them."

In the health arena, violation of personal space can deeply injure dignity. Mann explains that each culture defines an invisible space around the self and parts of the body that, if entered without permission, causes loss of dignity. Rape is an extreme example, but any inappropriate touch by a health care attendant may result in dignity loss.

Finally, the fourth type of dignity violation is humiliation. Mann reviews a spectrum of dignity violations from the more trivial doing "the wrong thing" in a situation (wearing the wrong clothes to an occasion) to a major violation such as leaving a patient undressed, exposed unnecessarily in front of others.

Mann reports that injuries to dignity provoke strong emotional responses including shame, anger, powerlessness, frustration, and hopelessness. And these violations are vividly remembered, with the act of recall restimulating powerful emotions even decades later. He concludes that health professionals need to understand that violations to dignity are sources of injury to well-being. Strengthening dignity is therapeutic and beneficial to illness prevention.

RELATIONSHIP OF WELL-BEING TO WORK

One way to connect the discussion of dignity and illness to the discussion of dignity and work is via the concepts of power and self-actualization. When patients and inmates in Mann's examples became invisible and lost all of their power to act, their dignity was denied. In the workplace, when employees lose their ability to act on their own behalf and work under conditions of widely unequal power, their dignity is compromised.

There is a wonderful set of social science research on the nature of work and human personality. Melvin Kohn, a leading figure on this subject, has documented 14 job conditions that clearly affect personal development. Self-actualization, a central factor for personal growth, reflects how much opportunity exists for an employee to use initiative, thought, and independent judgment at work.[15]

In order to activate initiative, thought, and independent judgment at work, employees need to perceive themselves as capable of such action, and employers need to confirm this capacity. This interaction mirrors the dynamic interface Mann described as central for dignity: the quality of how I see myself and how others see me.

Simone Weil's testimony provides a window on how specific conditions at work can injure dignity in all four categories. First, she reports "not being seen" by her employees as capable of self-direction. Her highly routinized job greatly restricts possibilities for exercising initiative. Next, she is not only invisible as an individual but also is rendered invisible by being lumped into the group category of "factory worker." Although a highly intelligent woman, Simone's talents and skills remain unseen by her supervisors. Her personality, her individual dignity is subsumed entirely into a group classification, in her case a group that is not deemed valuable. Third, in Simone's testimony, violations of safety to personal space occur regularly. The conditions at work do not insure her well-being, and all day she is subjected to risk of injury. There is little she can do to protect herself, and such vulnerability undermines her dignity. Finally, in her own words her deepest loss of dignity comes from humiliation. Her humiliation comes not from the physical discomforts and danger but from the contempt of her supervisors, their constant reprimands, and their demonstrable lack of respect for her. They are not interested in her desire to understand, to invent, and to think—that is, to be a person. Where there is no opportunity for self-direction, to paraphrase Kohn, people cannot thrive.

And Simone's humiliation is deepened by a sense of docility that overwhelms her. As a woman used to acting on her own behalf, this inability to fight back produces in her words a "falling into degradation," a loss of self. Simone's story presents a human face to the concept of being treated like an extension of a machine, a cog in the wheel of production.

Increasingly since the industrial revolution, human beings have become just another set of resources. Human resource or HR offices in corporations manage this set of resources in relationship to the bottom line. How people are treated, according to organization theorist Joshua Margolis, remains "contingent upon their contribution to firm performance."[16]

THE THREE PILLARS OF DIGNITY AT WORK

Let us now return to the Genesis story. When Adam and Eve began the first chapter in the saga of human work, there was lots to do. They had to till the soil to stay alive and to begin crafting a livelihood. There was endless opportunity for self-direction in naming the world's fruits, vegetables, and animals, producing children, and trying to create some order from chaos in the garden. There was a clearly named Sabbath day each week for rest and reflection. This time-out from regular work allowed a different kind of recreation and self-fulfillment to occur. And finally, the early descendants of Adam and Eve soon learned the lesson that it takes a joint commitment to build a tabernacle, trek through a desert, and reach the promised land!

The three pillars that uphold dignity at work remain the same for later descendents living in the twenty-first century:

To gain livelihood for oneself and one's family.
To have self-respect.
To "make a difference" through social responsibility.

The achievement of dignity rests on all three pillars—if any one is missing, the structure wobbles or collapses. Yet, for too many of us something is missing—insufficient income or job security to assure a livelihood; a lack of respect from superiors or of options to use our skills; no opportunity to make a contribution to society.

A focus group of generation X young professionals met in a Utah suburb not long ago and spoke of their difficulties in gaining dignity at work.[17] A young man in his twenties was worried about livelihood: "The key thing is, I'm making, right now, what my dad made for most of my life growing up. And he owns his own house, he has a lot of things that there's no way in the world I will ever own on what I'm making now." Despite a robust economy this young man saw himself skidding, facing a future of downward mobility, and had little faith that he could reverse the course.

A mother of two young children was concerned about how to maintain her self-respect as a mother with her paid work roles: "My husband is working. We don't own our home; we don't own a boat or any of those luxuries. We have only one car, and it's old, and we have two children. Now if we want to have just one more child, just in order to make ends meet and pay our bills, which we already can't do half the time, I would have to work full-time. But if I go to work full-time, then there's no point having another child because I won't be there to take care of her. And we do not have money for the day care we'd need."

And a 30-year-old pediatrician, who seemingly had put the dignity pieces together, quietly spoke up about reconciling his social responsibilities with personal needs: "I sense that more and more people are having difficulty making ends meet. More wives and mothers, single mothers working. All of us are working harder. That trend has had a dramatic effect on the children I see as a physician . . . and ironically, I think that is going to affect how much time I have to spend with my own kids, because I'm taking care of other kids' problems." At the end of the day, this young doctor felt the tremendous time demands of his work made him a lesser father.

❖ ❖ ❖

As we begin a new century, these young adults are joining older generations of workers in the widespread search for dignity at work. They are entering a world that is in the midst of major sea changes in gender roles, work expectations, and future visions. The time-money trade-off is a major theme of the group interviews I conducted with generation X and Y members. There is little expectation of job loyalty, and there is no job for life: "We are carrying our skills on our backs." They are like modern Bedouins carrying their economic survival tools from place to place, hop-scotching from firm to firm.

Those in their twenties and thirties know that the whole idea of what is productive is changing. "We know our parents' way of working no longer applies. For us, productivity is not measured by the number of hours worked but by the quality of the work we produce."[18] And the whole time and space relationship of working is radically shifting as technological changes allow a 24/7 time clock and an explosion of off-site locations where work can be conducted.

In this book, we will listen to echoes from history and to current voices of Americans regarding the three pillars of dignity: the economics of livelihood, the psychology of self-respect, and the political and spiritual dimensions of making a difference through social responsibility. Each of these pillars has its own composition and meaning. To understand our prospects for dignity and freedom, we need to explore each of the pillars. Then we will turn to two stories, one of employees searching for dignity at work and life in the evolving world of banking, the other of men and women on a similar search in the bumpy, ever-changing world of biotechnology. When we meet these people, we perhaps will catch a glimpse of ourselves in the midst of the same search.

We have already met four people who provide clues for how to move toward dignity: Kate, the lawyer, who is cutting back from overwork in order to have more time for the things she values; Dan, the accountant, who switched industries so he could use more of his abilities; Joan, the home health care aide who went back to school to get more education so she could get a better job; and Judith the domestic servant, who discovered that being an invisible worker meant relying on your own internal resources.

In each case, the movement toward dignity was a private event, occurring without change in the corporate culture or transformation in the larger economic paradigm. But without such major institutional shifts, each personal movement toward dignity, while courageous, was partial. Each of the four individuals still faces obstacles to achieving full dignity at work. Individual changes can therefore provide important steps forward, but larger institutional change is necessary for fuller advancement. We shall return to the question my daughter raised that helped to launch this book: "Mom, can you work and have a life?" From the time of Adam and Eve this has not been an easy question nor is it today. But it fuels the search we have begun.

CHAPTER TWO

Livelihood

The primary impetus to work is to earn a living. While other motivations for working, such as self-fulfillment and commitment to the common good are important, work that does not achieve a livelihood undermines human dignity. This is why the United Nations' 1948 Declaration of Human Rights was so clear in its insistence that human beings have not only a right to work, to free choice of employment, and to just and favorable conditions of work, but also to "protection against unemployment" and "to an adequate standard of living."

Nearly 40 years after the 1948 Declaration, the Catholic bishops' pastoral letter *Economic Justice for All* urged efforts for greater economic justice in the face of growing income gaps. Based on a ten point guide, the letter stated that "all people have the right to secure the basic necessities of life (food, clothing, shelter, education, health care, a safe environment and economic security)."

Achieving a livelihood for many Americans has gotten harder despite all the new technological advances, the increase of dual incomes for households, and the booming economy marking the last decade. American workers today labor more hours annually than do workers in any other developed nation. The difficulty in achieving a livelihood reflects numerous economic forces. These include the escalating costs of securing basic necessities, the continual expansion of the consumer necessities culture, the erosion of public-policy safety nets, and the inability of many Americans to find stable employment to pay their bills. In the quest for a livelihood, we have not spent enough intellectual capital on the question of how we can organize work so that it enhances family life and civic investment.

DESPERATELY SEEKING LIVELIHOOD

A group of small business owners sat around a table on a cold November day in Vermont to discuss their work lives.[1] The moderator began with the question "What defines a quality work life?" And almost simultaneously, one word hung in the air—independence. "Yes, independence—having your choice in terms of how to spend your time, who you spend it with, where you put your energy."

The conversation went on with people proclaiming the good American virtue of self-employment and the possibilities that open up for spending more time with family, on community matters, or communing with nature. Even for those working 12 to 14 hours a day, there was a strong sense that they had more freedom, more flexibility to construct time for things they wanted. "I used to work for a corporation, and you can't wait until Friday comes. When you work for yourself, you say, 'My God, it's Friday already.' And the summer—before I could not remember summer. Now there is so much to take advantage of in the summertime."

But soon the discussion took a turn to the darker side. The small business owners quietly began talking about their worries. "You think about whether you can keep up your quality of life. You really budget your money if you look at the $8,000 for taxes, another $5,000 for health care. And then you have to eat."

"And the cars, you realize you cannot keep up with the cost of collision insurance; they keep raising the deductibles . . ."

"And the health insurance, it just went up 17 percent!"

"Even if you have it, maybe it doesn't help. My friend just had a heart attack, and he's going to be paying the costs for years, because he's an independent person with only semi-insurance. And now they put him on a waiting list because his insurance may not pay for the transplant he needs."

"And there is no way to retire . . . not enough savings, no one else to look after me."

Among this very resourceful group of Americans, there was a sad recognition that, though they had worked hard and honestly for many years, they were still having a desperately hard time keeping up with the necessities of life. The specter of a future of accumulating expenses and insufficient livelihood hung over their independence dreams.

The small business owners in Vermont were not alone in seeking a livelihood that would provide security for themselves and their families. Factory workers in Tennessee were glad to be working in an automobile plant that offered relatively good job security, given previous experiences with layoffs: "As far as what contributes to my quality of life, I would say job security. It contributes a lot to my family life. In the past it has always been stressful, where we didn't know when we were going to be laid off." Another said, "What makes living good is a pretty good feeling of having a long-term job. Your future seems a lot brighter than [those of] people that don't have a good paying job, always worrying what could happen tomorrow."

What was most important to a group of low-income women gathered in a community center in the heart of an East Coast city was their endless quest to gain a decent livelihood for now and for later. These women struggled daily with trying to get and keep a job that would get them out of poverty and give them hope that they could offer their children a better future. This quest for a livelihood could be heard in their remarks. "I want to live in the same house for five years, to save money. But the cost of living won't allow me to do this. You can't live in this city and rent an apartment for less than $800 a month, and that is without any utilities. And then having children—the costs of day care are overwhelming." And, "I have a son. I don't want him to be where I'm at. I don't want him not to be able to do things because he can't afford to do them. I just don't want him to have to deal with the financial struggles."

There is a thread that weaves these voices together, voices from rural America, the suburbs, and the city, voices from women and men, from different ethnic, racial, and age groups. As the clock edges their lives forward, they want a guarantee that they will have access to a livelihood. But will the future world of work provide such assurance?

A GLANCE AT THE PAST

In the early days of the industrial revolution, workers were experiencing a very new way of working. As late as 1880, nearly half of all Americans still lived on farms, deriving their livelihood from agriculture. Yet, more and more folks were coming to the cities and mill towns to seek work. Single girls left farms to send money home to their families, just like the immigrants making a way in their new homeland. Young boys and girls, who never knew a life outside of the factories, all orchestrated their lives according to the bells that sounded out the workday.

In her rich descriptions of mill life, historian Tamara Hareven brings the voices of the past into sharp relief.[2] "I was brought up in the area of the mill . . . We didn't know anything else existed, really . . . We lived near the mills, we carried dinners for our parents (to the mill) and we were just accustomed to the mills," remarked a former male spinner. Hareven notes that few workers had any alternative to factory work, once arriving in a mill town either as a result of an end to a journey or by virtue of having been born there. "It was the way I earned my living; it was like a trade," recalled a lifelong textile worker.

"Nicer" white-collar type jobs did not pay as much as mill work. So, at the turn of the century, thousands of young people switched from the Woolworth's, ice cream parlors, and stenography desk jobs to the factory. Immigrant workers in particular were attracted to the regular pay and decent housing. The fear of poverty was deep for newly arrived immigrants who wished for pieces of the American dream: education for their children, a home of their own, advancement up the ladder of success.

To stand a chance of reaching their dream, working-class and immigrant families depended on the collective effort of women and children joining husbands and fathers at work. While American culture in general censored employment for married women, nearly one out of four women in the mill town Hareven studied worked in the mill. For single women ages 15 to 24, the figure jumped to three out of four! If a child was old enough to work in the mill, beginning at 12 or 13 years, this was welcomed as additional help. But young children posed a major problem for families trying to maintain their economic security. Some families were fortunate enough to have supportive extended family—grandmothers, sisters, aunts—to help out. Or sometimes it was an older sibling. "My mother said she always had 'one in the crib and one in the oven,' so it was pretty rough on her. When I was little, she worked in the [mill]. She'd leave one of my sisters, who was 12 or 13, in charge of us." Others without family support "loaned their children out for a week at a time, bringing them home on weekends, and paid by the day for someone to look after their children, or if they could not afford such arrangements, put them temporarily into orphanages."

One hundred years ago, life was a harsh struggle to gain enough livelihood to support a family. A U.S. Bureau of Labor Statistics examination of mill workers' family budgets give us a glimpse of what it was like to piece together a living:[3] A cotton bleacher, age 27, and his wife, age 30, a textile worker who worked only six weeks a year, earned $1,066 annually, of which $102 was the wife's earnings. The couple, who had children ages 4 and 5, spent:

Food	$457.79
Clothing	$219.84
Housing	$114.00
Fuel and light	$53.46
Furniture	$145.13
Miscellaneous	$212.78

The family was in the red at the end of the year due to a $137 doctor bill that could not be paid off. The better-off families tended to have three incomes, with the husband, wife, and at least one child working. The least well-off were the families with young children.

Hareven's account offers one slice of work and family life a century ago. There were those who made more money and those who were not even welcome in factories. But the mill workers were the solid backbone of the turn-of-the-century American working class.

A half-century later, the better part of a worker's life continued to be dominated by the need to earn a living. Seeking and maintaining a livelihood remained the principal theme for the auto workers studied by Ely Chinoy, an eminent researcher of industrial organizations.[4] The automobile worker of the early 1950s still worked for the same pieces of the American dream held dear by those in the mills: a "nice little home," education—hopefully now a college degree—for their children, and enough advancement up the escalator of success to assure a secure future.

In the years immediately after World War II, the manufacturing sector was robust, the service sector was just beginning its ascent, and the information sector was not yet imagined. The car became another success symbol, and those who made the cars were seen as the core of the American workforce. The auto worker believed in the words of Eleanor Roosevelt: "What sustains us as a nation is the feeling that, if you are poor, you still see visions of your children having the opportunities you missed." For the auto workers who had come through the depression and war years, these words rang true.

Chinoy's interviews reveal that auto workers had to deal with tough work conditions—some alluded to their time in the plant as daily imprisonment—in order to make a living. The $50 to $60 a week earnings for those doing well in the plant was achieved at a clear physical and emotional cost. The tempo of the auto assembly line was set by the speed at which the conveyor was moving, and no one on the line could leave until a replacement came. In the voice of one auto milling machine operator, "the trouble is that the foreman just thinks that a man is a piece of machinery."[5]

In another study of auto workers during the 1950s, Robert Guest quoted a 36-year-old spot welder (who, with overtime, was pulling in just under $80 a week and had just bought his own home): "I don't like to work on the line. You can't beat the machine . . . The big thing is that steady push of the conveyor belt—a gigantic machine which I can't control. You know it's hard to feel that you are doing a good quality job." Yet, this same auto worker was clear there was nowhere else to go. "I'm scared to leave. I'm afraid to take the gamble on the outside. I'm not staying because I want to. You see, I'm getting good pay. We live according to the pay I get."[6]

Staying in the auto plant, like staying in the mill, was the best livelihood option in town for most workers. And in the 1950s many of these workers saw pieces of the American dream become a reality. By the end of the 1950s, over 60 percent of Americans owned their own homes compared to 43 percent two decades earlier. A 39-year-old welder Chinoy interviewed who had lived in a slum said, "We're all working for one purpose, to get ahead . . . My next step is a nice little modern house of my own. That's what I mean by bettering yourself." And a nonworking, skilled maintenance worker with 14 years plant seniority commented, "A lot of people think getting ahead means getting to be a millionaire. Not for me though. If I can just increase the value of my possessions as the years go by, instead of just breaking even or falling behind and losing . . . and put some money away for when I can't work . . . I'll figure I got ahead quite a bit."[7]

One of the big differences between the mill workers and auto workers was the replacement of the household network by the male breadwinner model as the means to attain a family livelihood. While the cultural mores had always promoted the primacy of women in the home, for most families women had also played an important role in sustaining the family income. Like women and children on the farm, members of a mill household banded together to produce a family income that could sustain livelihood. In the intervening years, the concept of the family wage finally came to fruition. Married women were prohibited from many jobs and, after the Rosie the Riveter era, were forced to leave the World War II jobs they had held.

THE FAMILY WAGE

The concept of a family wage represented cultural attitudes about both economic livelihood for the family as a unit and gender relationships between husband and wife. Specifically, the family wage promoted the idea that a sole male breadwinner should provide for his family, and his wife should manage the home.

Historically, this idea first emerged in the mid-1800s and was forcefully supported by the growing trade union movement at the end of the nineteenth century as a way to increase inadequate wages and help families rise above a marginal existence.[8] By the early 1900s, the inability of many full-time workers to provide their families with basic necessities intensified arguments for a living wage. A Colorado daily newspaper expressed the opinion that male wages should allow the male worker to "keep his wife and children out of competition with himself and give them the same opportunities for improvement and intellectual and moral training and comfortable living as are enjoyed by those who do not labor."[9] This early version of the living wage effort echoed the family wage argument for suitable wages for male heads of households.

Thus, the family wage idea linked together preferred patterns for wages, family, gender roles, and ideal images of "true womanhood" and the "real man." This ideal also provided a new definition of childhood, the evolution of a new age group called adolescence, and new labor laws protecting youngsters. According to the family wage concept that became a basic assumption for business and labor in the United States, employment of married women was thought to lower wages and thus to undermine both male livelihoods and the true order of wife-husband relations.

The separate sphere culture—men in the public sphere and women in the private—supported by the family wage outlook not only emphasized the inherent dangers of women's employment, but also provided the rationale for different levels of pay for similar work and for differing minimum pay levels for men and women. The family wage supporters also made women's important unpaid labor invisible by stating that a man alone can support his family. The care-giving activities and other domestic roles done mostly by women were discounted from official family budget reports.

Moreover, the reality that there were households headed by women was left out of the equation.

By the end of World War I, the family wage concept was embraced by working-class families, economists, public agencies, and the business and labor community. The concept responded to and supported working-class sentiments to raise wages, especially given the absence of welfare systems. This was the era before social security systems and public safety nets had been put into place. And, the concept supported those advocating gender divisions for work and family.

But while the demand for the family wage had many supporters, the corresponding reality did not emerge. Research suggests that the family wage was not widely achieved by male workers, and during the 1940s "there was a dramatic change in the structure of the American family wage."[10] The entry of the United States into World War II brought an end to the true family wage, with the proportion of adult women with earned incomes growing from 39 percent in 1939 to over 60 percent in 1966.

ANYONE HOME

The family wage idea did surface a deeply troubling current in the sea of changes affecting work and life in America. Who was responsible for the care giving, unpaid work on the home front? If indeed it was the wife and not the husband, then the rising tide of women as wage earners posed a major threat to conventional thinking. And who was responsible not only for cooking the proverbial chicken in the pot but also for taking the time to buy the pot?

To achieve a livelihood by the 1970s, most American families were relying on two incomes. The 1970s equivalents of Ozzie and

Harriet were both working outside the home in order to have a home, to send their kids to college, and to pay for their escalating health care. Measures of the declining reality of the family wage are informative: Today the family wage is calculated by a family wage ratio in which the median family income with a wife in the paid labor force is divided by the median family income of a family without the wife in the workforce.[11] The resulting number shows to what extent the economy is based on a true family wage system (the ratio would be 1) or true wage equality between men and woman (the ratio would be 2). Between 1951 and 1969 the rate was between 1.25 and 1.31. Harriet probably had a part-time job, and Ozzie continued full-time. After 1980 the ratio increased at a fast pace, reaching 1.69 in 1993. And the rate has continued to inch up, to 1.72 in 1998. By then, Harriet was also working full-time, but often at a lower paying job. As a number of economists have noted, this movement partly reflects the declining earnings of men in certain income groups rather than simply a rise in women's wages.

But though this may ignite cheers from those supporting women's equality, the question of who is taking time for the home front remains. In the words of Randall Tobias, CEO of Eli Lily Corporation, "a good business cares about both the intelligent mind and the anxious heart of the employee."[12] If an employee is worried about the child left unattended at home, the parent needing to be driven to the doctor's, a sick partner, then both productivity in the workplace and the dignity of the worker will suffer.

Thus, today's typical family solution to gaining a livelihood—two folks working harder than ever—has benefits and costs: It has advanced certain choices for certain women. Many women, especially single parents heading households, have little choice but to work wherever they can find jobs. Few real choices have opened for men. According to the Bureau of Labor Statistics in 1999, of all married couples with children under six, only 3.3 percent had a "stay home" dad. Some working-class couples have organized shifts so that one parent can be at home to take care of the kids. However, most men remain tied to the old breadwinner model which denies options for assuming equal care-giving roles.

It has also raised new problems for connecting livelihood and dignity: Can dignity at work be achieved only at the expense of the unpaid, caring work front? Deborah Stone's thoughtful research on home health care documents that informal care giving can be a full-time job.[13] Studies of patients with common chronic conditions such as Alzheimer's and Parkinson's disease find that informal care givers devote anywhere from 20 to 70 hours a week caring for them. Day in and day out, a child with ear infections or asthma, an adult with a bad back or in need of chemotherapy treatments also needs someone at home to help. With two people working, there is no one at home to cover these ongoing responsibilities.

Our paid work efforts undermine our basic dignity if there is not time to fulfill the unpaid labor at home. When we set a criteria for a successful livelihood, it includes coverage of unpaid caregiving work. And to uphold values of equity, the criteria need to be applied universally so that success for men and women in gaining a livelihood is measured similarly.

What to make of these profound and disturbing changing tides and questions?

A response emerged during a 1996 focus group of retirees living in Florida.[14] They were talking about their work and their struggle to have a decent life. "I think all of us are children of the depression era. So we all, at some point, experienced what it is like to be poor. But we did not think we were poor, because everybody was in the same boat. By the time after the war [II], we had children. We had a pretty reasonable financial status, so that our children had everything they needed. They had their education, their clothes, whatever they needed in the home. We mothers also had more time to spend at home with them than do parents today." This was a story of the post–World War II success of the family wage. But these elders in America were very concerned about what they saw going on in the present. "No one is home. The kids watch TV and play the computer by themselves. How can this be good for the children and for the family and for building good values? A good life means earning a good living and having time for living."

A few years later in a 1999 focus group, a group of seniors in college were speaking about their future.[15] A young man was pondering his future livelihood. "I really want to be involved in raising my kids, that's really important to me. I think that if you're going to commit yourself to having a family, then you should do a good job of it. I do not want to sacrifice making a good living, so it will not be easy."

So both sets of seniors, in Florida and at the university, saw the connection between achieving dignity in paid and unpaid labor. The older generation composed their lives in reaction to the Great Depression and were grateful for the security of their families and their modest possessions. The generation Y youngsters had lived a fancier lifestyle but in a vivid way felt poorer than their elders—not cared for enough, not enough time with their families. They wanted a win-win solution that would allow them to feel rich in both the paid and unpaid parts of their lives.

But there are major challenges to a successful pathway, a direction that will integrate the fulfillment of a decent livelihood with time for caring at home. The dictates of a bottom-line culture based on the competitive global market push many of us into a no-win situation.

GROWING INEQUALITY

When I was a little girl, we use to play a game called high water–low water. A rope was held across the ground, and after getting in a line, we would take turns jumping over the rope. At first the rope was low to the ground, assuring that everyone could make it over. But the rope was gradually raised, and as it rose higher and higher, more and more children could not make it over the rope and became losers. By the end of the game, only one or two were winners.

At the end of the 1990s, many Americans still found themselves unable to afford the basics of the dream: home ownership, college education, and full health care for their families. The bar had been raised, preventing individuals and families from entering the winners circle. After adjusting for inflation, between 1989 and 1999 prices at public colleges increased by 22 percent and at private colleges by 28 percent. At private institutions, the average cost of tuition, room, and board increased to 42 percent of median family income in 1995. In 1997, about 3 million working family households earning between $10,700 a year (the equivalent of a full-time job at minimum wage) and 120 percent of area median income (about $75,000 in Los Angeles, for example) paid more than half their incomes on housing. During the early 1990s, one out of four Americans had a lapse of health care coverage, and nearly 40 million Americans were uninsured. In the United States in 1996, nearly 11 million children were not covered. By 1997, in the midst of a booming economy, 21 percent of low-income children were uninsured.[16]

There is no magic formula for staying out of poverty in the United States. Even working full-time is no guarantee: Almost 7 percent of couple-headed families with at least one full-time worker are poor. Single-parent families are twice as likely to be living in poverty, even when the parent (almost always a mother) is working full-time.

For the working poor, the basic elements of the American dream are out of reach. For example, while the housing policy in this country for the last 50 years has been based on the premise that if you work, you should be able to afford a home, a 1999 study documents that a full-time employee earning $7 an hour cannot afford an average-priced, two-bedroom apartment in any state of the union.[17]

While the number of professional and technical jobs has greatly increased, so too has the number of low-skilled, low-paying jobs that often come with no benefits. And as Harvard University economist Richard Freeman laments, "it is shameful that 'prisoner' is just about the fastest-growing 'occupation' in the United States, the 'trade' of more than 2 percent of American men."[18]

During this decade, a small number of Americans found themselves with new levels of wealth. A typical CEO of a large U.S.-based corporation in 1992 was taking home $3,842,247, a 56 percent increase in one year! Between 1960 and 1992 the average salary of a CEO jumped $3.6 million. The gap between high and low earners, which had been relatively stable during the 1950s and 1960s, accelerated through the 1970s and into the 1990s. For example, in the 1970s men in the top 10 percent of the earnings distribution earned, on average, 90 percent more than the median wage in America; by 1995 this had increased to 120 percent. For those in the lowest 10 percent, the gap from the median earnings went from 120 to 140 percent. Women earners on the top and bottom mirrored the male pattern.[19]

In my home community of Lexington, Massachusetts, a contentious issue for the Town Meeting was the "mansionization" of local housing. Modest, affordable houses were being bought up by developers, only to be torn down and replaced by much larger, expensive mansions.

Lexington is the Revolutionary War town where the "shot heard round the world" for freedom occurred. Originally a farm community, it evolved over two hundred years into a mixed-income location where small business owners, service professionals, and high-tech scientists intermingled. By the 1990s, the town had a large number of elder citizens on fixed retirement incomes who worried about the increasing costs of schools, water, and waste disposal. Many of their children, who had grown up in the town, were being shut out of the home market by the rising costs: The average price of a home in Lexington rose from $32,000 in 1970 to $210,000 in 1990 (more than a six-fold increase compared to household incomes that did not even double). The destruction of perfectly good housing to make mansions sent a ripple of distress through the community. Would the town only be a refuge for the rich in the future, raising the bar too high for middle-income families?

The fact of growing inequity of income in the United States in recent decades has been well documented. During this time period, how well you did depended a great deal on where you began. For example, the median wage of males working full-time for a full year increased 25 percent between 1963 and 1973 but declined slightly (5 percent) between 1973 and 1987. If you were on the bottom, you fell even harder than those above you. But if you found yourself in the ninetieth percentile, your wages actually rose—rather than declined— 12 percent from 1970 to 1987! There was truth in the phrase, "the rich get richer," and those on the bottom fell further behind.

The boom on Wall Street through the 1990s further widened the income gap. The household income for the poorest fifth of American families rose less than 1 percent from 1988 to 1998, but it jumped 15 percent for the richest fifth. This translated to income for the poorest households averaging $12,990 before taxes for the period, while the richest households averaged $137,480.

Back in the good old days of the robber barons, even J. P. Morgan, the icon of capitalistic greed, ruled that the CEOs of his companies could not earn more than 20 times what the hired workers earned. By 1980, the average CEO was earning 42 times that of the average worker. In 1998, CEOs at the major companies earned 419 times the pay of the average worker. In the same year, CEOs' pay increased by 36 percent while workers received an average pay hike of 2.7 percent.[20]

Economist and business leader Marina Whitman, in her cogent book *New World, New Rules,* outlines several explanations for increased earnings inequality. First, the value of education has increased. In 1979 the average male college graduate earned about one-third more than the average high school graduate. By 1993, an average male college graduate earned 70 percent more in wages than their high school counterpart. High school graduates had a clear wage advantage over high school dropouts.

But Whitman points out that the education premium accounts for only one-third of the total increase in the widening wage inequality. Another important factor is skill-based technological change. Some economists think that this change significantly accounts for the shift in labor demands, diminishing the job and earnings prospects for the less skilled. Other factors include an increase in global trade, a decline in the value of the minimum wage, and a decline in unionization.

The increase in global trade has affected the flow of both capital and labor to serve markets around the world. Since World War II, multinational corporations have abandoned the restrictions of national boundaries and increasingly buy and sell goods and employ people anywhere, anytime. By the 1980s, the computerization of work meant that information could be transformed instantaneously around the globe and at low cost.[21] With fast and cheap information exchange, customers and laborers could be found in any location. For example, a doctor in a Chicago hospital could relay his patients' records to a transcription service, who, in turn, would send his notes electronically to a low-cost operation at an offshore site in the Caribbean. This global transaction would wind up cheaper than paying higher wages to Chicago-area workers.

An estimated 10.3 million workers are minimum wage earners, of whom 60 percent are women. One-third of these workers are parents of children under 18 and include almost a million single parents. A full-time worker earning a minimum wage will earn $10,712 a year, well below the 1998 federal poverty level of $13,000 for a family of three.

The value of the minimum wage has been decreasing in the last two decades, so that it is now 21 percent lower than it was in 1979. Congress, according to the provisions of the 1938 Fair Labor Standards Act, is in charge of approving increases of minimum wages. Without new increases, the real value of the minimum wage will fall to $4.67 an hour (in 1999 dollar terms) by the year 2003.

The decline of union membership in the United States is dramatic. "In 1955, approximately one third of the American labor force and a majority of the hourly workers employed by large corporations were covered by collective bargaining agreements. By 1995 only 16 percent of the overall labor force and less than 11 percent of the private sector labor force were organized."[22] Historically, labor unions have been a chief organizing force for fair and better wages.

While questions remain about which factors most influence wage inequality, there is little doubt that they interface in ways not easily understood. But one thing is clear: Having skills and an increased knowledge base is a key to success in the future economy. And the competition today is not on the local or even national level, but rather operates on a global playing field, so the very top folks get more and more and others fall to the wayside. It is like the high water–low water children's game—a field of few winners.

RUNNING HARDER TO STAY IN PLACE

In trying to get into the winner's circle, many Americans have found themselves in a race against time. Like the characters at *Alice in*

Wonderland's tea party, folks are running harder and harder just to stay in place. But, of course, this is not a fictional story; it has real costs for families and communities across our nation. People interviewed in focus groups from across the nation shed light on this reality:[23] "We have got a situation where there is a time famine in most people's lives, and you have to have a deliberate strategy to prevent your life from being overwhelmed by it," said a professional computer worker in Seattle. A twenty-year-old health worker in Salt Lake City said, "Our workplace is the most important thing. My coworkers, who are in their twenties, can spend 50 to 60 hours a week in the workplace—that is where their time is, that's where their life is."

"I think there are changes in society where people have to work a lot of overtime," said a fast-food worker in North Carolina. "And I think that this is both positive and negative. I mean, I think for the family it has very negative repercussions. I think it's very hard when you don't have one parent there—male or female. I guess the positive is there is more equality between the genders than there was 50 years ago. But I think for families, it's negative."

Perhaps the concern raised by people most often is the lack of time for taking care of loved ones. Many workers feel their schedules are full, and they have to find time to spend with spouses, children, parents, other relatives, and friends. Unlike the 1964 Rolling Stones' song, a worker does not feel "time is on my side, yes it is!"

In our society, we have not paid serious attention to the costs of doing business as usual. How do we add up the costs of lack of time to care for children, to pay attention to elderly parents, to invest in community activities? David Hamburg, the former president of the Carnegie Foundation puts it this way: "Thus far, we've done things on a small scale [mediating work-family demands], and whether we can scale up remains to be seen. It would take some kind of national commitment, with all the sectors involved. But if we pull all that together, we could do a lot to reduce the damage now being done."[24]

Gaining a livelihood did not always completely dominate life. As economist and social commentator Juliet Schor has described in her important book *The Overworked American*, it is a myth that capitalism has reduced working hours. The modern 40-hour work week, when compared to the nineteenth-century 80-hour work week, may look good, but in pre-industrial times the workday rarely exceeded 8 hours. A typical workday in medieval times included periods for breakfast, lunch, and dinner; a time-out for an afternoon nap, and even midmorning and midafternoon refreshment breaks. The medieval calendar was also chock-full of holidays that included not only long vacation times around Christmas and Easter and midsummer, but also embraced numerous saints' days and rest days. It is estimated that leisure time made up about one-third of the entire year!

The great gains of free time touted as a result of the rise of industrialization are thus illusory. With the rise of new technology, especially marked by the invention of the clock, work became redefined. Time became equated with money, something to be saved, bought, or sold. As E. P. Thompson noted, time became "currency: it is not passed but spent."[25] Labor time, rather than just labor, is what counts.

By the nineteenth century, "for whom the bell tolled" had clear meaning for the mill workers. The system of having bells signal workers when to arrive at work, when to eat, and when to end the workday had begun in the fourteenth century, when the first public clocks were installed in textile towns in Europe. At first, workers tried to silence or control the bells, which were mechanically rung, but fines and penalties were enforced by employers and city officials against the rebels.[26] The workers' activities became regulated by the clock, and work life has not been the same since.

During the twentieth century, concern about long workdays grew, sometimes leading to appropriate public and private reforms. One example of public reform was the Fair Labor Standards Act of

1938, which codified the eight-hour workday. This was thought to be a beginning step to better balance the increasing demands of the industrial age with nonwork aspects of life. In addition to setting up the eight-hour day, the 1938 act also required an overtime premium to discourage the use of overtime in place of incremental hiring of new workers. However, because employers' contributions to social security, unemployment insurance, and other benefits are capped after a certain earning level, they prefer to require extra hours for existing workers rather than hire new ones. Thus, employers see it less costly to require extra hours, and the overtime premium has not been an effective barrier.

An excellent example of private reform was the Kellogg Company's experiment with the six-hour day. In December 1930, Kellogg president Lewis Brown ordered the replacement of three daily eight-hour shifts with four six-hour shifts. By adding a shift, he hoped to create jobs for the unemployed during the Great Depression. The experiment attracted much national attention, and for years people saw Kellogg as leading the way to a "future when free time would replace work as life's central concern."[27]

Although the employees at Kellogg held on to some form of the six-hour day until 1984, the vision of a society where leisure replaced work never was realized. In fact, by the 1990s, many scholars were writing about overwork and double-burdens and "three jobs—two people." While opinion varied about how many hours Americans were working, there was wide agreement that, indeed, the average American was working more in 1990 than in 1970. This was startling, given the premise that new technology and a more productive economy were supposed to result in more leisure, not more work!

One explanation came from economists Barry Bluestone and Stephen Rose. They argued that many Americans were both over-worked and underemployed: Because of growing job instability due to temporary layoffs, downsizing, and other job losses, employees worked as much as they could, when they could. In some cases, people were working two or three jobs to meet the livelihood needs of their families. They cited the fact that 70 percent of workers in a Chrysler plant were working extra hours most weeks to keep up with costs of food, housing, and car payments.[28]

Their view is substantiated by a recent survey by the Kaiser Family Foundation which says that two out of five families report sending an additional family member into the paid labor force or having an existing working member take an additional job simply because the family needs extra money.

The stress of extra hours for many workers is compounded by the extra burden put on most families. As the Sloan Foundation's Kathleen Christensen and Ralph Gomory note, "the fundamental arithmetic of the family has changed . . . In today's two-career family, there are three jobs, two paid and one unpaid, but still only two people to do them."[29] They call on Americans to adapt to new formulations of the workplace and home.

THE BALANCE OF LIFE

American people share a sense that something is amiss on the economic front but are searching for the words to describe it and the solutions for another way. They want an economy that assures growth with security, achievement with fairness. According to a commissioned survey by the Merck Family Fund during the 1990s, people of all backgrounds believe that materialism, greed, and selfishness increasingly dominate American public life. These forces are seen as crowding out more meaningful values centered on family, responsibility, and community. And disturbingly, while 85 percent of the respondents rate these values extremely high, they believe that less than half of other Americans agree with them!

Strikingly, 86 percent of those surveyed feel "today's children are too focused on buying and consuming things" and are distressed about the future of an American dream defined by purchasing and "keeping up with the Joneses." But they are ambivalent about change. According to the survey report, the respondents want it all: material security *and* a commitment to a quality life for themselves and the nation.

Achieving a livelihood and a meaningful quality of life has been traditionally posed as an either/or equation. From its inception, the emphasis on materialism—brought about by the successful development of capitalism—has been accompanied by new forms of social distress. An early example is the effect of the enclosure law in Elizabethan England. Land where the poor could build huts and eke out a living was taken by the landed gentry for sheep grazing since wool had a high market value. This resulted in a new class of "wandering poor," a consequence of the market-driven process.[30]

THE COSTS OF ACCUMULATION

Adam Smith, the famous father of capitalist thinking, was clear about the social costs of the accumulation impetus. Because of the emphasis on multiplying the productivity of labor in order to maximize output, the manufacturing process was divided into many separate steps. The resultant division of labor saved time and encouraged worker dexterity. But Smith also saw the costs to the workers. "The man whose whole life is spent in performing a few operations has no occasion to exercise his understanding . . . and generally becomes as stupid and ignorant as it is possible for a human creature to become."[31]

In Smith's vision, the processes of capitalism would bring about increased earnings for many. For those it did not, Smith saw a role for government to address the moral considerations of society. And significantly, he believed that the push for relentless growth would stop when society had "all the capital it needed."[32]

However, Smith foresaw neither the impact of technological change nor the erosion of moral concerns in public life. It was Joseph Schumpeter during the Great Depression who named "creative destruction" as the process propelling capital accumulation. Creative destruction pushes for the displacement of older products by new ones and the displacement of workers no longer viewed as economically useful. Large corporations that always need to change and expand output and markets encourage this displacement. Thus, the market economic forces are wed to a culture of planned obsolescence and expanding consumerism. The culture of consumerism, in turn, supports the rise of values of greed, materialism, and selfishness decried by Americans today.

The critical turning point for Americans regarding consumerism came in the 1920s. Emergent manufacturers realized that a livelihood attached only to meeting basic needs would not enhance the push for mass production. Thus, an enlarged American dream was created, a dream that was a moving target, so that when a family reached one level of affluence, it would aspire to the next. The promotion of "more is better" and "newer is the best" supported the work-and-spend sequence Americans have adopted.[33]

There was some resistance by labor groups and social reformers, who wanted the increased productivity to be turned into more leisure time rather than a cycle of longer work hours and more consumption. For over fifty years, the struggle for the eight-hour day was led by unionized artists, craftsmen, and female factory workers. They saw leisure time as necessary for family life, community participation, and spiritual development of the individual and the country. But the business arguments won the battle.

Since that period, America has indeed become a very wealthy nation, raising the material standard for the majority of its citizens while increasing the inequality between the rich and the poor. Simultaneously, most Americans, especially in the 1980s and 1990s, are working longer and longer hours to keep up. And the average American is consuming twice as much today as Americans did 40 years ago. This drive for accumulation is hotly encouraged by an enormous advertising effort. During the last decade about $150 billion was spent annually on advertising in the United States. This is approximately the total amount the nation spent on higher education.

The tension between materialism and an ethical life existed early on in American history. John Winthrop, the Puritan colony's first governor, understood the difficulties of restraining material desires and pursuing moral values. During his voyage to America in 1629 on the ship *Arbella*, he gave his famous speech warning that economic interests could prove overwhelming. He cautioned the arriving settlers to make certain that the "good of the public oversway all private interests."[34] Prices, wages, and markets were to be regulated for the good of the commonweal.

The notion that material wealth is to be held in moderation was a strong early American ideal. By the mid-1700s, colonists were criticized for "generally failing in their duty to the community, seeking their own aggrandizement in the rich opportunities afforded by the land, commerce, crafts and speculators."[35] The simple life was esteemed as the societal ideal.

Down the Atlantic coast from the Massachusetts Bay, the colony founded by William Penn linked faith to moderation. The early Quakers believed that wealth itself was not evil, but luxury and greed were. "Riches serve wise men, but command fools." The Great Awakening movement, beginning in the 1740s and lasting a century, called for Quakers to renounce their growing affluence and return to a life of simple living. John Woolman led this effort by forcefully speaking out on the effects of commercial success on family and community life.

For Woolman, simplicity had economic virtues as well as spiritual benefits. Dignity of work was a central value: Lowered consumption would lead to more workers producing necessary goods, not luxuries, and workdays would be shortened so that work would not be endless toil but a source of pride. The pursuit of work was seen as feeding the soul of the individual and the soul of the emerging nation.

But the fast growing economy in America pressed hard against the fabric of simple living. By the time the industrial revolution hit full force and Americans flowed to the cities and factories, the moral arguments that held together the simple life were mostly ignored except by those on the margins. By World War I, folks were ready for the Roaring Twenties, Schumpeter's creative destruction, and a consumer culture aided by unparalleled advertising.

EXTERNALITIES

The costs of this turning away from a connection between the livelihood and the spiritual well-being of the individual citizen and the nation have rarely been measured by economists. Economists in modern times have almost exclusively turned their attention to standard market system mechanisms and processes, whether local, regional, or global. As noted economist John Kenneth Galbraith points out, his one-time Harvard colleague Schumpeter never focused on the costs of creative destruction, "including the possibility of painful recession or depression."[36] This is comparable to a doctor touting a new miracle drug without listing any of the possible side effects.

All the factors concerning our state of well-being or quality of life are called "externalities." Unlike the "internal" costs of labor and raw materials that are factored into regular cost equations, externalities are not seen as relevant to the process, to the assessment of productivity. Any costs of externalities are foisted onto individuals or communities who are external to the production process itself. For example, the environmental costs of global warming, the costs to families of long work hours, the health costs of unemployment are not measured as an integral part of production.

The market mechanism and the economists that explain productivity do not, therefore, accurately fulfill their responsibility of giving "society an accurate assessment of the relative costs of producing things." An example provided by Robert Heilbroner provides a close-up snapshot of the inaccurate picture that emerges if externalities are not taken into account: "Suppose, for instance, that there are two ways of making steel, one of which is very clean but expensive, and the other dirty but cheap. Competition will push producers to choose the cheaper way, and an unsophisticated observer will say that the market has thereby helped society increase the efficiency of its operations. It could be, however, that if the laundry bills and health costs were added into the production cost, the cleaner process would turn out to be the cheaper."[37]

In the above instance, without factoring in the externalities of cleanup and health care, a more complete and accurate assessment of efficiency is lost. The market is meant to guide resources to their most rational use. However, what the market and most economists hold as the criteria for rational use is the maximization of profit, not public good. While these may not always be a zero-sum equation, until externalities are carefully factored into the central equations, an accurate picture of the costs and benefits of our market economy will be missing.

BRINGING EXTERNALITIES INTO WHAT COUNTS

In the beginning, Adam Smith spoke out against the external costs of mind-numbing work routines such as those experienced by the textile workers in the mills, by Simone Weil in her factory, and by Ely Chinoy's auto workers. At the end of the twentieth century, we heard the voices of elderly seniors and college seniors regarding the external costs to children and family life of having two parents with three jobs. Looking at externalities in a serious way provides a window on the difficulty of achieving dignity at work in the current economy. But it also provides an opportunity to rethink the roots of the market system and reawaken efforts to achieve an integration of livelihood and well-being for individuals, families, and communities. Adam Smith in his writings demonstrated a concern for linking accumulation of wealth with an improved standard of living. Efficiency, as currently used, is a biased term. It covers up the costs of doing business as usual.

We need to start putting into our mainframe economic equations the real costs of doing business. In the current equation, all profit-making activity is seen as good for growth while all other nonprofit activity is seen as unproductive. But common sense tells us this is absurd: The spilling of oil by the *Exxon Valdes* is counted as good for our gross national product, while the unpaid care-giving activities of millions of Americans (mostly women) is not counted in the equation.

We need a new economic equation that counts and values what is productive for our lives, for the well-being of our families, and for the viability of our society. This is not a position against economic growth, but rather a question that asks growth by whom, for whom? More specifically, the issue is efficient for whom, productive for whom?

At this challenging time, as a new global economy is emerging, we need and deserve new economic thinking and tools that bring together new ways to measure what we value: a new economic equation that connects the ethics of human dignity with an agenda for the economy. The either/or formulation that pits dignity against economic measures is no longer viable, no longer acceptable. The costs are too high for too many, and we can do better for ourselves and the future generations.

A RIGHT LIVELIHOOD

If we think that the quest for a livelihood and a meaningful life are connected, then new definitions are necessary. In 1995 the Radcliffe Policy Institute launched a New Economic Equation Project that was based on the following challenge: What would an economy look like if work was organized to enhance family life and community life? A few years before, across the ocean in Italy, a national women's organization called The Cherry Orchard proposed a new law to make time for work, the schedules of the community, and the rhythm of life more humane. Their proposal began, "Everyone needs time to study, to work, and to care for others and for themselves."[38]

The call for a "right livelihood" has a strong history. In the United States we have seen that early political and religious leaders such as John Winthrop, John Woolman, and William Penn called for moderation in the economic way forward. In this century, the term "right livelihood" has been most promoted by Gandhi as part of the Indian liberation struggle; Dorothy Day and Martin Luther King, Jr., in the poor peoples' movements; English economist E. F. Schumacher in relation to new technologies; and nonviolent activists primarily concerned with human dignity. Simply put, right livelihood unites the quest for a livelihood with the quest for social justice.

Gandhi is usually thought of as a great political and religious leader. But much of the success of his leadership for national liberation was due to his thinking as a development economist. A very poor country, India needed a vision for livelihoods that would provide resources for nation-building to the people. Gandhi asserted that what India needed was "not mass production but production by the masses." He pushed forward a plan for "good work," a process that encouraged individuals to achieve a decent livelihood, while developing facilities for common community tasks and goods and services needed for a sustainable nation.

One highly successful example of good work in India was the very pragmatic program of refusing to buy British textile products, in much the same way the Boston revolutionists had thrown tea overboard. Before British laws outlawed homespun cotton, India spun and wove in cottage industries, creating a livelihood for the masses. As a bold move to gain livelihoods and national independence, Gandhi led a boycott of British goods and encouraged the spinning of cotton cloth by millions of people all over India—men and women, elders and youngsters. This campaign recognized that as long as India was dependent on Britain for producing cloth, it would not gain independence. Achieving economic independence from Britain and building labor skills for people were linked in the spinning of cloth in thousands of community marketplaces. This realization of good work discouraged meaningless endeavors and offered a way for people to be gainfully employed while making a contribution to the nation. It is notable that, under this example of a right livelihood, people could experience a real sense of initiative and control over their daily work while contributing to the nation's economic growth.

An economist very impressed with Gandhi's good work formula was E. F. Schumacher. He promoted a new way of thinking about gaining a livelihood under the term "Buddhist economics." This thinking proposed that since consumption is merely a means to human well-being rather than an end in itself, "the aim should be to obtain maximum of well-being with the minimum of consumption."[39] Thus, it imposed a self-limiting aspect to achieving a livelihood, reflecting Buddhist philosophy. In Schumacher's vision, industries and communities would be planned according to a human scale, and the technologies sought would be appropriate to human values. This intermediary technology was preferred to other forms of technological innovation since it would be cheaper, healthier, and more satisfying. It would allow more fulfilling work and leisure. Under this form of right livelihood, labor would be considered an output rather than an input and thus measured in a different way.

Schumacher's *Small is Beautiful* achieved bible status to many in the United States who were struggling to create a positive alternative to the inequalities in American life and to the social, environmental, and psychological costs of growing materialism and a global market economy. A long and distinguished list of thinkers including Lewis Mumford, Paul Goodman, Barbara Deming, C. Wright Mills, Daniel Bell, and David Riesman spoke up against the shallowness of a consumer culture.

And some folks went to live the good life. Scott and Helen Nearing began "a simple, satisfying life on the land, to be devoted to mutual aid and harmlessness, with an ample margin of leisure in which to do personally constructive and creative work."[40] They saw their hard labor on the land as exhilarating, for they were their own bosses, and their life was enriched by aspiration and effort "rather than by acquisition and accumulation."

Fellow nonviolent activists Wally and Juanita Nelson began a homesteading lifestyle on about three-quarters of an acre of a land trust in western Massachusetts. Their values led them to do work that would "do no harm" and provide for their basic needs. Juanita shared her experience of a right livelihood: "The primary purpose of the plot is to provide our own food as the basic and most easily accomplished step to becoming as self-sufficient as we can manage, disentangled from getting our living from a system built on injustice (a big mouthful of a reason to have a garden, and sometimes I'm ready to eat those words)."[41]

Wally and Juanita saw their way of gaining a livelihood as performing a service of getting food to others and thus allowing them to claim a share of the production and service of others. This reciprocity was essential to their own dignity and to the dignity of others. Their way of life, living a right livelihood, connected good work with a healthy society, connected personal independence with freedom for all in our nation.

A right livelihood is not easy to establish in our current market system. The people who have chosen to reach for it include internationally recognized leaders, such as Gandhi, and local, inspirational people, like Wally and Juanita.

The challenge of gaining a livelihood is not one-size-fits-all. For poorer Americans, it is just getting on the first step of the pathway leading to job security. For many workers, it is gaining enough economic stability to insure the basic pieces of the American pie. For others, it is the continual battle of never feeling there is enough, that one is not successful because there is always the need for more.

What unites these diverse groups is the general sense of unease reported at the start of this chapter. Americans are indeed experiencing the costs of the externalities of the current economy, including increased family stress, a sense of loss of time, environmental decline, emerging violence among children, and financial insecurity. Concepts such as good work may be old-fashioned, but the human desire to achieve a livelihood and embrace a meaning-

ful existence remains. And a right livelihood—that unites livelihood with social justice—is a notion that deserves much more
consideration.

CHAPTER THREE

Self-Respect

> She seeks wool and flax and works willingly with her hands
> She is like the merchants' ships; she brings food from afar
> She rises also when it is yet night, and gives meat to her
> household and a portion to her maidens.
> She considers a field and she buys it; with the fruit of her
> hand she plants
> A vineyard
> She perceives her merchandise is good; her candle does not
> go by night . . .
> She stretches out her hand to the poor; she reaches out her
> hands to the needy.
> She makes fine linen and sells it to the merchants.
> Strength and honor are her clothing and she shall rejoice in
> time to come . . .
>
> —Proverbs 31

This woman, an early supermom, gives us a vivid picture of a life where work provides not only a livelihood but also self-respect. She reaps strength and honor from her paid and unpaid labors: We see her skillfully working with her hands; we see her diligence and commitment to feeding her household; we see her intelligence at work and in the market place and we see her reaching out to those who are in need. She has composed a life that gives her inner strength and validation by others. It is a work life that most of us seek to replicate, work that offers us dignity resting on internal respect for ourselves and the respect drawn from others. And like the Woman of Valor, we could all use more sleep and recreation time!

The unrelenting competitive thrust of the market economy and the current organization of work in our society present major challenges as we seek self-respect. Adam Smith, as the father of modern capitalism, understood the consequences of the division of labor and its deliberate separation of mind and body. In Smith's famous example of work in a small pin factory, we see how, by dividing the manufacturing process into small separate tasks, ten men could produce 48,000 pins per day rather than 200 when each person did a whole pin individually. But setting up work so each person did mindless, repetitive tasks resulted in people "becoming as stupid and ignorant as it is possible for a human creature to become."[1] Dignity, thus, is difficult to achieve in industrial society because of its exclusive concern with economic efficiency.

DISRESPECT AT WORK

In the movie *Modern Times,* we witness Charlie Chaplin's silent tramp being dehumanized by the dictates of the machine. The tramp is a factory worker whose job is to tighten nuts and bolts on an endless series of machine parts. The key to his job is to perform his movements and tasks with clocklike tempo and precision.

In a great opening scene, from his station on the assembly line, the tramp holds wrenches in each hand to tighten nuts on a long stream of steel plates carried on the conveyor belt. The foreman urges him all the time to keep up with the belt. When he itches for a moment, makes a gesture, or brushes away a troublesome fly, he causes tremendous chaos for fellow workers down the production line. He is always frantically rushing to catch up and restore order. In the film, the tramp is fighting a losing battle. He can never keep up. He cannot restore order to the line, and eventually, he can no longer restore order to himself. He becomes a "nut" and is sent away to a psychiatric ward.

This undermining of self-respect at work has also been a theme in major sitcoms on television. In the 1950s we watched plumber Art Carney and bus driver Jackie Gleason on *The Honeymooners* battling disrespectful bosses and customers, and we saw Eve Arden as a high school teacher on *Our Miss Brooks* being treated like a mindless idiot. By the 1990s, we watched professional workers—doctors on *ER,* lawyers on *LA Law,* police detectives on *Hill Street Blues*—wrestling with the stresses of overwork, insufficient resources, corrupt officials, and, again, disrespectful bosses. We watched and often laughed because we understood, we empathized with their dilemmas.

Since individual dignity and fulfillment in a modern society is closely linked to our work, our economic order is not performing its social job. Opportunity to achieve self-respect through work is seen by well-known business scholar Peter Drucker as shrinking. "The realization of human dignity would thus emerge as the major unanswered question of industrial society."[2]

DEFINITIONS OF SELF-RESPECT

As one of the pillars of dignity, self-respect is understood as something produced internally by a person. A picture emerges out of a small well of dignity deep within each of us that can be drawn up when needed. However, others have come to see respect as a dynamic process—a result of interaction between people. A person's dignity, therefore, exists and is replenished depending on interactions between an individual and the larger world.

Sara Lawrence-Lightfoot has spoken of respect as a dynamic verb rather than a static noun. "Respect is commonly seen as deference to status and hierarchy . . . By contrast, I focus on the way respect creates symmetry, empathy and connection in all kinds of relationships."[3]

This dynamic understanding of respect builds upon the insight of philosopher Martin Buber, who sees in every human encounter the possibility for growth. Buber describes two basic different forms of human encounter: I-It and I-Thou. In the former, an individual regards other human beings from a distance, as part of the environment. In contrast, when an I-Thou relationship occurs, the individual approaches another with his or her whole self and enters a true dialogue. Buber sees this authentic connection as a reflection of a human meeting with God.[4] When human beings hold each other with genuine respect, that relationship has a wholeness—some would even say a sacredness.

From a less religious, more psychological perspective, Judith Jordan describes the relational aspects of self-esteem. Our culture's frequent preoccupation with competition leads to a concept of respect based on who is better than whom. To move away from a competitive model of respect to a relational one involves "trying to feel good about oneself (by forming) good connections and to be empathetic."[5] Having a sense of commonality with the other person is central to giving and gaining respect. In this sense, Jordan offers a version of Immanuel Kant's reasoning that people share dignity.

Many of us struggle at our daily workplaces to get the r-e-s-p-e-c-t touted by Aretha Franklin and embodied by Proverbs' Woman of Valor. As psychiatrists Jean Baker Miller and Irene Stiver suggest in *The Healing Connection,* in relationships of unequal power commonly found in the workplace, it is difficult to establish the interaction, the mutuality necessary for achieving self-respect. But they maintain that power differential does not preclude mutuality. "Mutual empowerment is very different from a power-over way of operating. As a basic shift in thinking, we can unlink the concept of power from the concept of domination. The power of people to interact so that both benefit is unlimited."[6] Just as parent-child, student-teacher relationships can foster a connection that enhances each person's capacities and sense of themselves, workplace relationships have the potential to do so as well.

PERSONAL IDENTITY AND WORK

Do workplaces support connections that encourage self-respect? Most workers, indeed, do not hate their jobs. On the contrary, many polls continually demonstrate that people report being satisfied with their jobs. University of Chicago psychologist Mihaly Csikszentmihalyi notes, in a recent study of 170,000 workers in 16 nations, 83 percent of white-collar workers and 77 percent of manual workers indicate job satisfaction.[7]

And in 1955, sociologists Nancy Morse and Robert Weiss did a survey asking male workers if they would continue to work if they inherited enough money to live comfortably without working.[8] Eighty percent said yes. They concluded that working is more than a means to a livelihood for the overwhelming majority of those employed. The meaning of work for almost all of us goes beyond the paycheck.

The relationship of work to job satisfaction and self-esteem is not, however, one size fits all. Experiences vary depending on one's occupation. For example, the Morse and Weiss study reported that individuals who were in middle-class occupations emphasized the intrinsic interests in their jobs and the sense of accomplishment that came from work well done. Individuals in working-class occupations emphasized the necessity of having activity to occupy time, mind, and body. For farmers, demarcation between work and the rest of life was blurred; thus, most farmers could not even consider a life without work.

Moreover, the study revealed an inverse relationship of job satisfaction and wanting to be doing something else. The less prestige a worker experienced at a job, the less the worker desired to continue the same type of work should luck strike enough to inherit a fortune. In other words, while most workers did indeed wish to continue their work, the majority of traditional blue-collar workers and low-skilled service workers wanted to switch jobs. Most often they wished to go into business for themselves. This response indicated a desire for a job with more autonomy and more prestige. These factors—the ability to have more control and say at work and the capacity to gain external validation—can be seen as a quest for greater self-respect on the job.

There is a vast collection of wonderful literature on the search for respect at work all along the occupational continuum. In a classic study, *The Hidden Injuries of Class,* Richard Sennett and Johnathan Cobb reveal the pain and alienation of those who are not getting respect in their jobs. We start at the middle of that status ladder, paraphrasing the Christopher Robin poem, either half way up or half way down the stairway.

George Corona, a senior foreman in an aerospace firm, is a middle-level manager struggling for respect at his workplace. He sees himself as a little "above the drones" and far below the scientists above him. His aerospace job places him in a no-win position. He needs to see that everyone under him produces, but he holds most of them in contempt—they are not worthy of respect. But he is dependent on them to make his job possible so that he can please those above him, who do not give him real power. He is caught between those he disrespects and those who disrespect him. In the end, he is left with disrespect for his own work. He thinks, if only he had more ability and drive, he could have been a scientist. He feels he is personally responsible for his loser position: "If I had really developed my science, I wouldn't be involved in such a situation . . ."[9]

In a close-up portrait of the inner-city world, where people experience alienation and a life condemned to the margins of society, social scientist Philippe Bourgois provides another tale of the ongoing search for respect. Two of the main subjects of the book, Primo and Caesar, wish to make it in the legitimate service sector, filled with white-collar professionals. But the cultural clash between their "scrambling jive" way of life—the way they look, talk, make sense of things—and professionally acceptable behavior is too big for them to overcome. Primo tries to hold on to a mailroom clerk job at a downtown professional trade magazine. His attempt to succeed at the office ends with his deepening humiliation. Primo explains: "I had a prejudiced boss . . . She would like to talk about me to whoever was over visiting in the office . . . you know, like her associates who would come over for a coffee break. When she was talking to people, she would say, 'He's illiterate,' as if I was really that stupid, that I couldn't understand what she was talking about."[10]

In the office world, Primo becomes an invisible man. His boss talks about him to others as if he does not even exist. He is "dissed" in public as if he is not there to hear the disrespect. This invisibility causes a profound unraveling of Primo's self-worth. This is reminiscent of the earlier example given by Jonathan Mann of the deep shame caused to hospital patients when doctors discuss them as if they cannot hear, as if they are not present. It pushes Primo to make a rational decision to escape from a world where he can't get respect to the underground economy. There he is not subject to a constant erosion of self-esteem. "Ray [a street drug dealer] would never disrespect me that way, because he wouldn't tell me that because he's illiterate, too. Plus I've got more education than him, I almost got a G.E.D."[11]

When the connection between doing a good job and being seen as doing a good job does not exist, there are costs to the individual employee and often to the product or service involved. Writer Suzanne Gordon, in her interviews with nurses, vividly describes their chaotic work climate. A nurse working in a major city hospital reports, "From day to day, you didn't know which unit you were going to work on. Especially on the weekends. You would be floated from unit to unit . . . There were never enough nurses. Nurses were so demoralized that they were always calling in sick or leaving. You'd be taking care of twelve or thirteen patients all by yourself."[12]

In the hospital setting where both the nurses' sense of dignity at work and the care patients received suffered, nurses were being treated without the respect they deserved. As Gordon notes, administrators who supervised the nurses and the hospitals which employed them generally viewed nursing as a low-skill profession, which anyone could do with a little training. This devaluing partly reflected the fact that most nurses were female and that care giving in general is not valued; it is not seen as "productive" in our society. The nurses thus were granted little respect, their work conditions undermined their own sense of respect, and as a result they became demoralized. The value of their work was invisible. The connection between doing a good job and being seen as doing a good job was severed.

Such insidious invisibility is often a by-product of the kind of racism described by Barbara Neely in her mystery novels through their heroine, Blanche White, a black domestic servant. Through Blanche's eyes we see the relationship between white women employers and black servants. We see how an intelligent, resource-ful, and often brave person is viewed as an object of derision rather than a subject of respect. Like Primo, domestic servant women have to rely on their own inner resources to overcome a world of work that offers them disrespect. The question for them is from where do they replenish their well of dignity?

Finding self-respect at work is an ongoing dynamic. Dignity is not static, something that becomes uncontested once attained. For those most on the margins, the search for respect may rationally lead to attachment to the world of the underground economy. For those trying to get up the approved escalator of success, the struggle can also be difficult if not as hard.

Slightly up the ladder from Primo and Blanche are the fast-food workers in America. They experience the daily struggle of trying to develop self-respect in a highly stigmatized job. Society devalues their job, and each day at work they come into contact with the customers on the other side of the counter who think nothing of "dissing" them. And, at work, they are trained to not talk back but to smile and to give the customer respect. How then do they cope and maintain self-esteem?

Anthropologist Katherine Newman's insightful research on fast-food workers in New York's Harlem explains that fast-food companies teach employees to redefine the situation by playing on the most basic definitions of dignity in the United States. "Hey, *you* have a job. The fool who is dissing you across the counter probably doesn't. You're part of the mainstream. They are not."[13] This sacred division in our culture—between those who work and those who do not—is the key. While the fast-food workers may be on the bottom step of the success escalator, they are on the escalator. Their sense of self-respect largely comes from identifying with others higher up the escalator and looking down on those off the escalator. Thus, Katherine Newman's inventive title to the fast-food workers' story, *No Shame in My Game*. It is a defensive but proud statement. You can claim self-respect because you have crossed the river as wide as any in America—crossed over to the side of being a worker. These workers become part of the very American ideal of making it through work. Rather than being a subculture, the fast-food workers are trained to see themselves as part of the mainstream.

But being on the bottom rung is not easy. And the fast-food workers know they have a long way to go. They continually have to be reinoculated against losing respect and being badly treated. They know dishing out french fries puts them at the bottom of the heap, and that in itself is wounding. So they live a hard balance of looking down on the jobless and looking up at all the others who have better jobs.

TRYING TO CUT BACK AND KEEP RESPECT

For those who have been on the upper end of the occupational continuum, the self-respect issues are different. They involve decreasing loyalty between firms and professional workers, diminishment of control over decision making, and changes in time demands. For example, physicians have traditionally been attached to the medical profession in large part because it offered autonomy, financial reward, high job security, and status. By the year 2000, however, more physicians than ever were leaving medicine for other careers. The emergence of managed care has caused disillusionment among doctors and their patients. Physicians, who are opting out of a career that once assured self-respect, report that they have less time for patients, more grunt work, and less intellectual stimulation, as their work becomes increasingly controlled by insurance companies interested more in profits than in medical care. "Society in many ways has devalued medical practice," says a former radiologist at Massachusetts General Hospital.[14]

Doctors are not the only professionals in the respect struggle. We met Kate in chapter two who is losing respect at work as she moves to being a part-time lawyer. Going slower professionally also has clear costs. Lawyers are all trained to uphold a standard of "face-time" on site and commitment. When lawyers choose to alter this standard and go part-time—even if they have always been seen as good workers—their devotion to their profession becomes suspect.

The part-timers themselves internalize the lowering of respect. "We found that some attorneys we interviewed were quite harsh with themselves and expressed self-doubts about their role as a professional. They became ambivalent about their performance and questioned their worth."[15] One former part-time lawyer felt she did not measure up to "a professional standard that professional self-worth should be measured by constant availability, desire for partnership, and doing the 'sexy' deals."[16]

Going against the accepted professional norms can exact a price on an individual's self-respect. The respect given by others, including family and friends, may also diminish. In the case of going part-time in a profession where the politics of time at work shape success, reduction of hours is seen as wrongdoing. It is taking yourself off the up escalator in a culture where going up is the name of the game.

In the United States approximately one out of six workers is employed part-time, and 70 percent of those are female workers. There is little respect given to part-time work in general, and benefits are nonexistent for many who hold these jobs. Part-timers are viewed as not really trying to be successful, which is labeled immoral in our culture. With professional part-timers, there is relative disrespect. They are in the professional club but at the lower end. Club rules are harsh. Not making the most of yourself is seen as countercultural. "The possibility of failure is the most uncomfortable phenomenon in American life. There is not room for failure in our schemes of respect."[17]

The guilt and disrespect the part-timer feels are real. The rules of the firm are clear, and if you do not play by them, you are penalized. Thus, even though part-timers may choose fewer hours for good reasons—such as realizing family values—they lose respect at work. The trade-off may be worthwhile but not easy and not without loss.

WHEN WORK DISAPPEARS

A different kind of loss of respect is experienced by those who lose their jobs. In my own studies conducted over the past 20 years, I have interviewed those out of work due to plant closings, dislocations, reengineering, and downsizing. Through the eyes of those who have lost their jobs, we see how important work is in our society for self-respect.

During the early 1980s, many workers in America who thought they had it made in the major industrial corporations of auto, steel, and aircraft found themselves unemployed. Like my father, they had done everything right: worked hard, done a fair day's work for a fair day's pay. But through no fault of their own, they found themselves cast out of work. And even though they were unemployed because of economic decisions not in their control, they felt personal shame for their failure to hold a job.

Earl, a 63-year-old drop-hammer operator, was one of the first laid-off aircraft workers I interviewed in 1981.[18] He was living in a trailer park across the street from the largest aircraft plant in Hartford, Connecticut, which had been his place of employment for 28 years. He had major hearing loss in both ears since all the shop supplied for noise was cotton, until the 1970s, when OSHA made headgear mandatory. Earl was laid off and waited to be recalled. When he finally was called to return to the plant, it was two weeks after his seniority rights expired. He became bitter and depressed as he faced loss of seniority, loss of pension savings, and a major cut in salary. His wife and children separated from him. Earl said with disbelief, "I put my whole life into the industry but they tell me, 'That's the way the cookie crumbles.'" He could not understand what had happened and kept asking what he could have done to prevent this. He wanted to feel that there must have been something that was in his control, that he could have done to save himself. Not finding an answer in the confusion, he blamed himself. The plant had laid off thousands of workers along with Earl, but he experienced the job loss in solitude. It was a personal failure to Earl that he had lost the work that gave him self-respect.

The personalization of job-loss experiences in the United States is common to many employees from many industries. The Horatio Alger myth is very powerful: the belief that if you rise up, it is due to your own efforts, and if you sink, it is due to your own failures. There is no powerful story that supports the view that an individual's job history reflects larger situational and organizational forces. In America the stories are private, based on the individual, not social or based on institutional contexts.

An interview I conducted with an engineer in the 1980s gives a close-up look at the length people will go to conceal what they consider the personal shame of losing work. It was in the midst of the downsizing of defense industries across America. In one year alone in Massachusetts in communities around Route 128, known as "defense–high tech highway," 14,000 employees lost their jobs. Wayne was one of the numbers. He had been a senior systems analyst and had a postgraduate education, a wife, and three children. When he lost his job, he did not tell anyone in his family. Each day he dressed as if he was going to work, and his wife packed his lunch along with the kids' as usual. He spent the day in the stacks of the public library. Wayne said, "Without a job, there was an empty feeling in my stomach. I had recently moved into a new house and there was no layoff notice. We were in financial jeopardy. I had trouble sleeping and trouble breathing. I didn't know who I was or where it would end."

Wayne knew that others like him had lost their jobs, but his suffering was solitary. He had lost his sense of worth, his sense of self to the degree that he could not even express his loss with his own wife or family. His shame cut him off from all others, which deepened his depression. Finally, a fellow unemployed engineer discovered him in the library and they began to talk, eventually forming a self-help group to pull themselves out of despair.

For both Earl and Wayne, it was as if they were falling down the up escalator they had been on. Somehow they had misstepped, unable to rescue themselves. Sociologist Robert Merton discusses the consequences of people feeling that the future, their security is out of their control.[19] This loss of agency, of being able to help one's self, leads to hopelessness and a loss of faith in social structures. When the cultural values of a society extol common success goals but a person is denied access to achieving these goals, anomie and deviant behavior result. This erosion of faith within the individual and toward societal institutions has dangerous private and social costs.

One particular externality that is usually not measured in the social costs of job loss is the effect on children. A number of researchers have provided strong evidence of the ways unemployment creates stressful change for families. These stresses include decline in both financial and social status, changes in family role patterns, and absence of security and hope for the future.[20] But few have looked at the more direct impact on children.

In the excellent book *Children in Crisis,* psychiatrist Robert Coles explores how socioeconomic issues are not just parenthetically important, but rather play a significant role in how children see themselves. As family economic losses increase, children are apt to think that others think less of them, which affects their view of themselves. Children are socialized by parents and taught in school that work and self-esteem are linked. Thus, when a child sees a parent lose a job, this linkage is called into question. This undermines the child's faith in the agency of the parent and calls into question the truth that work is something valuable.

Marienthal, a study of unemployment in an Austrian community in the 1930s, offers rarely collected data directly from children.[21] When the factory shut down in the village, the entire community was hit hard, and the authors report a widespread "breakdown of a social personality structure." For fathers in families, this meant an inability to be the breadwinner and loss of authority. For mothers, this meant compensating for the lost income from their own factory jobs and their husbands' jobs by producing more goods at home and working harder to keep the family going. Children responded to the skidding circumstances of their families by becoming more and more resigned to a world of scarcity. When the authors asked children to write an essay on "What I want for Christmas," the Marienthal children hesitated to ask for anything at all. The discrepancy between a child's wish and fulfillment was enormous, resulting in an environment of depression and unspoken embarrassment between children and parents.

In postdoctoral studies I did at Children's Hospital in Boston on unemployment and children's lives, I worked with doctors in the emergency room and family violence clinic. We found that a rise in unemployment rates in the metropolitan area correlated with a rise in child neglect, a rise in reported cases of physical abuse to children, and dramatically higher incidences of stress-related children's illnesses, especially asthma. Because health insurance is tied to employment in America, when a family member loses work, insurance coverage is also lost. If physical or mental illnesses develop, a family often puts off getting medical attention until a crisis occurs (e.g., a severe asthma attack), because going to an emergency room is the only solution. The costs to the well-being of family members and also to the larger community that often picks up the expensive emergency treatment are very real consequences that often are not counted.[22]

These health effects on children also included the loss of a child's self-esteem. Children who wanted to help their parents became frustrated and experienced a decrease in self-image. Younger children experienced guilt, wondering if something bad they did had caused their parents' misfortune. Longer-term unemployment was especially hard on children, causing them to feel shame in school when asked what their parents did for work. If the family became downwardly mobile, children lost their ability to go on class trips, play sports, or even keep their home. The entire family was caught by the escalating private costs of job loss while they had fewer resources to cope.

During family therapy sessions at Children's Hospital, deprivation was a common theme that surfaced among the children of the unemployed. As children participated in play therapy, their underlying worries and concerns emerged. One child drew a picture of houses upside down and trees with limbs missing. Another small child drew a self-portrait in which he was very tiny, with no arms or legs, and a father who loomed large and angry. One eight-year-old devised a castle from which she constantly looked for the king and where the queen was worried about money and where they might live when the castle was taken away.

Other researchers have studied the private and social costs of being out of work in America. Katherine Newman speaks of laid-off air traffic controllers as defining themselves as "damaged goods" and their attempt to reconstruct a reality that would permit regaining dignity.[23] William Julius Wilson compares the attitude toward job loss and poverty in the United States to that of European nations, with the former holding that "individuals are largely responsible for their economic situations," the latter favoring structural explanations such as "social injustice, misfortune or changes in the modern world."[24] The importance of being a self-made person is a very strong value in American culture.

Wilson provides a powerful argument for how job insecurity is connected to the lowering of agency, which he terms self-efficacy. Perceived self-efficacy, according to psychological theory, refers to beliefs in one's ability to take necessary steps to achieve stated goals. Unstable work and low income, Wilson hypothesizes, will lower one's perceived self-efficacy. Studies show that there are serious negative consequences on mental health and parental behavior from economic stress. Indeed, the substantive literature on the effects of unemployment provides clear evidence that the longer one is out of work, the more severe the private and social costs.[25]

Addressing the meaning of unemployment brings us back to the meaning of work. Examined from a variety of economic, social, and psychological perspectives, work is seen as providing a place in society, a sense of freedom, and a measure of sanity. The reality is that work has far more than financial consequences. It allows for connection between the individual and the larger society, and it shapes everyday life by giving a person a place to go, a sense of purpose. The instinct to do good work was seen by Thorsten Veblen as one of the deep strengths of American character.

WOMEN'S WORK: PAID AND UNPAID LABORS

It is important as we move into the twenty-first century to note the vast change in women's attachment to paid work over the last decades. The early supermom spotlighted in Proverbs is testimony that women have always worked. What has dramatically altered has been the relationship between paid and unpaid labor. This great transformation that unfolded as industrialization and urbanization took place in human history shaped the way work is done and what work is valued by society.

Increasingly, valued work came to be associated with work done outside the home—mostly paid work done by men. The respect given to unpaid labors at home increasingly diminished. As care-giving work shifted outside the home, it was perceived as less skilled work and not highly valued in the market economy. Therefore, jobs such as child care workers, elder care attendants, and home health care aides—jobs mostly held by women—were classified as low-skilled, low-pay positions.[26]

Women's place was seen to be in the home or, when women worked outside the home, in service or care-giving labor. One hundred years ago, only unmarried women could properly be engaged in industrial factories, and even by the 1930s the majority of states prohibited married women from school teacher positions! Freud and others saw women's lives resting on only one of the two pillars of human existence: love, not work.

By 1986, for the first time, a majority of women with children of preschool age—children as young as one year old—had paid employment. By the 1990s, three-quarters of all employed women were working full-time; 68 percent of married-couple families in 1998 were dual-income households. The average woman worker today can expect to spend 30 years in paid work, with long absences for child rearing no longer a reality. As we turn to the next century, the majority of new entrants to the labor force will be women, often immigrants and of color.

But despite fundamental changes in women's work patterns, women's work often has not been granted value and respect. A pay gap still exists, and women face difficulties in being promoted, exercising authority, and, in many cases, getting hired into nontraditional fields, such as construction and engineering. In 1996, women who worked full-time, year round earned 74 cents for every dollar earned by men. Over a lifetime of work, the average 25-year-old woman who works full-time, year round until she retires at 65 will earn $523,000 less than the average working man.

In my interviews with unemployed women from many jobs including those in the garment industry, the shipyard, nursing, teaching, and high tech, there was a common theme: no validation for the extent of their loss. These women deeply felt the importance of work in their lives, but when they lost their jobs, it was not witnessed by others as significant. Women said they did not receive support from others, in contrast to the support received after other life losses such as miscarriage, death of a loved one, or divorce. Friends would comment, "You now have time to do all the things you could not do before, like finish a pile of sewing or weeding the garden." Many husbands and partners were reported to be relieved that the woman would be at home more. For these women, there were few places to express the grief of losing work that was important to their lives and to their self-respect. Compensating with more time for care-giving work at home, which women already deal with more than men, was not a satisfactory solution.

The central meaning of work in women's lives has been ignored historically. During the Great Depression, major studies were done on the effects of job loss on individual and family well-being. The 1933 study *Ten Thousand Out of Work* did not include any women. E. W. Bakke's 1940 classic, *The Unemployed Worker,* also ignored women workers. While men felt shame when they lost jobs, the outside world saw their rightful place to be in jobs outside the home. A woman laid off from work was supposed to feel glad to finally be back in her appropriate role at home. This exclusion of women reflected the prevailing notion that women were meant to be at home, and if a woman entered paid work, she risked her health, her rightful place in society, and the welfare of her children.

This view of women's work has been resurrected in recent years during debates about tax incentives for homemakers and as justification for poorly paid care-giver jobs. For women, the struggle to integrate the demands of the paid workplace and the demands of unpaid labor at home remains ongoing. In a study I did on the meaning of work in women's lives, the words of one respondent summed up the sense of many. "My mother worked. My daughter will work. For your dignity and self-respect, you work. To be somebody."[27]

❖ ❖ ❖

The connection between self-respect and work is a basic truth of our culture. It is true for women and men in our society. In the quest for dignity at work, the questions remain: Who achieves respect and who does not? In the new world of work, will the achievement of self-respect be more or less difficult? During each of our life stages—since our lives and workplaces are not static—we may have different access to self-respect at our jobs. While writing this book, I had the help of research assistants who were juniors and seniors at college, members of generation Y. A resourceful student named Patricia told me about a song that had much meaning for her as she pondered her future, the choices about work and life that lay before her. The song, "3 Strange Days" by School of Fish, had a chorus that spoke to her about the struggle for personal identity and self-respect in a new world of work, where there is little loyalty and constant change:

> I had no obligations
> My mind was a blur
> I did not know what to do
> I think I lost myself
> When I lost my motivation.

Patricia was searching for a compass to help her compose a life where she could have it all: respect for herself, success at work, time for a quality life. A few days before graduation she got married, and a week after graduation she was off to her first job at a large international banking firm. Her fear was that she would make a lot of money but lose herself, lose a sense of respect for herself. Her hope was that she would keep up her motivation, keep a clear mind, and find work that would allow her to keep her self-respect. She wanted to be a modern woman of valor. The search for self-respect at work is a universal constant.

CHAPTER FOUR

Social Responsibility

Eating box-lunch sandwiches and chips, we were sitting around a small conference table down the hallway from the offices and labs of a major biotech firm. The men and women represented different occupations at the company—a human resource administrator, a few technicians from the manufacturing division, and a number of midlevel scientists. The company had agreed to be part of a case study on the biotechnology industry which, later in this book, will help to illuminate some problems and solutions for dignity at work.[1] Big things had just happened for the firm. A favorable Food and Drug Administration ruling on the clinical trials for a human cell procedure, which they had sweated over for the last months, had come through. They were not sure how this would affect their job security in the short run or long run, and the conversation turned to why each of them was working in biotechnology.

The theme of social responsibility emerged loud and clear. These technicians, quality control managers, scientists, and business officers shared a belief that their work in biotech made a difference in helping others. They saw themselves on the cutting edge of making discoveries that could improve the lives of thousands. A scientist began, "When I first started, I went into a basic research job where I learned a lot, but I felt far removed from actually helping somebody . . . but when I went into biotech, there was close affinity. So that was one reason why I came, everything else is second." Another 30-year-old technician spoke up, "In biotech, it's so new, I have no idea if this company is even going to be here for five years . . . But the simple fact of the matter is that I can sit here and say I came in and I helped to save this person . . . there is that type of job satisfaction."

Around the room there were affirmative nods and a general consensus that their work served the public good. The belief that their work contributed to the lives of others was a strong positive feeling that provided a counterbalance to the uneasiness of an uncertain job future. In this moment in history, when long-range job security is hard to find, making a difference can be the way to keep your dignity intact.

The commitment of biotech professionals and technicians to work of value mirrors research on the notion of professional ethics. In his book *Work and Integrity,* William Sullivan suggests that the very idea of professionalism has historically included a "broader, more socially responsible sense of calling."[2] Anne Colby and her colleagues report that three-quarters of executive, administrative, and managerial respondents in their study of American workers bring at least some concern for social responsibility to their work.[3]

The voices of biotech workers, who are employed in manufacturing, service, and information-knowledge labors, raise interesting questions about the third pillar of dignity at work: social responsibility. For the biotech workers, the feeling of doing work that is of use to others seems to provide a concrete way of offsetting the downside of a world that offers decreasing job stability. Is this a conscious trade-off many of us find attractive and within our reach?

HISTORICAL ROOTS

The idea that work has a social purpose has roots both in our nation's history and within various religious traditions. In early America, most citizens were self-employed producers, whether on the farm or in the cities, where work, family, and community roles converged. Commenting on family life in Plymouth, historian John Demos describes how the household was the locus of all institutions, serving business, educational, religious, judicial, and welfare purposes.[4] These social functions connected households to the rest of the community in a daily, integrated way so that household prosperity and prosperity for the community went hand in hand.

In our nation's first years, Jeffersonian democracy was a response to the question of how personal drive for success was best reconciled with concern for social welfare. Jefferson thought that democracy itself rested on the active participation of citizens in the social and political sphere. For Jefferson, the ideal occupation was the citizen farmer who could make a living while contributing to the larger community. He was very concerned about the separation of self-interest from community service: "If people forget themselves in the sole faculty of making money, the future of the republic is bleak and tyranny would not be far away."[5]

Frenchman Alexis de Tocqueville in the 1800s questioned what institutions filled the gap between the individual and the state in American society. Could work fulfill private ambition and the common good? His response was that in America this gap was largely filled by voluntary associations on the local level. Membership in these associations within communities across the society were the primary way Americans generated and experienced a sense of responsibility for the public good. He, like Jefferson, flagged concern about the emphasis on personal ambition, often found in the workplace, that makes people "forget their ancestors . . . clouds their view of their descendants and isolates them from their contemporaries."[6]

With the rise of industrialization, the definition of success increasingly was framed in very individualistic and material terms. The Horatio Alger stories of self-motivated success (or failure) became the prime narrative for life and livelihood. Achievement of success was cut off from the context of family and community connections and a moral base. Terms of success were reduced to material gains that could be easily measured in quantitative ways. This isolated view of success undermined the traditional ideal of a figure like the town father who achieved status by connecting self-motivation to service to the community. Instead, Adam Smith decried the bad effects that commercialism was having on human higher aspirations, "The minds of men are contracted, and rendered incapable of elevation. Education is despised, or at least neglected, and heroic spirit is almost utterly extinguished."[7]

For the majority of Americans living in urban and suburban settings, work, family, and community life became separated. Integration of individual success with social responsibility became more difficult. The National Advisory Commission on Civil Disorders, addressing the problems of poverty and unemployment in the troubled cities of the late 1960s, summarized the significance of linking work to social purpose: "The capacity to obtain and hold a 'good job' is the traditional test of participation in American society. Steady employment with adequate compensation provides both purchasing power and social status. It develops the capabilities, confidence and self-esteem an individual needs to be a responsible citizen and provides a basis for stable family life."[8]

The work life of a person is seen as setting forth not only a prognosis for individual livelihood, but also a prognosis for family and social values. However, in today's fierce economy, work has become separated from these values and instead is driven by the economic bottom line.[9]

❖ ❖ ❖

One counterforce to this movement a century ago was the rise of professionals who viewed their work, at least in part, in terms of social effects and social responsibility. The social attachment professionals traditionally have had to their workplaces was very deep, coming after prolonged training that strongly encouraged commitment to the professional community. Personal satisfaction derived, therefore, not in isolated terms but rather in relationship to the larger work community. The professional community, in turn, through its specific set of expertise met its mission of serving the community at large.

Traditionally, the work of most professionals was shaped by the social support provided by others in the profession. Sociologist Robert Merton noted that professionals were not isolated as they performed their tasks.[10] The individual lawyer, for example, was not required to settle cases exclusively on his own reading of the situation, but rather by referral to preexisting professional codes or others' interpretations of the codes. Librarians in towns and cities around the nation counted on professional associations for setting up standards and combating censorship pressures. Current conditions for professional workers, however, provide evidence that a major gap exists between the ideal of professional life and the reality. Today many professionals experience conditions that erode social support in the workplace and distance them from the social values that motivated them to join the profession in the first place.

A notable example is what has happened to doctors, one of the most respected professions in our society. With the bottom-line culture of managed care taking over medical policies and practices, many doctors have felt their ethical commitment to their patients seriously compromised. They have experienced the professional dilemma of having to choose between providing appropriate care for their patients and meeting the cost demands of health insurance companies. In reaction, some have given up their practices to become part-time salaried workers, some have begun to organize doctors' unions, while others, as we saw in chapter three, have left the profession completely. The doctor's battles have been focused on their working conditions. Dr. David Christiani, a Massachusetts General Hospital physician who has led a doctors' union says, "The bottom line was quality of patient care . . . Doctors were being distracted from direct involvement with patient decision-making activities."[11]

Historically, not just professionals have had a calling to social responsibility. Another counterforce to the separation of social responsibility from work has been the movements of labor organizations. Workers in the trade union movement have often tied their struggles in the workplace to larger societal issues of equality and social justice. For example, female operatives in the turn-of-the-century factories were among the leaders for a shorter work week that would benefit adult and child laborers.[12] In this century, sleeping car porters pressed for racial justice and fair wages, and farm workers pushed for better environmental protections from workplace hazards and better health care for all.

More recently, auto workers in a Saturn plant won paid community release time from their jobs to help rebuild churches that had been burned down in outbursts of racial hatred and civil unrest. Other paid community release programs in unionized workplaces and sometimes in nonunion firms have allowed employees to build low-income housing, engage in literacy efforts, and care for AIDS infants in hospitals. The rich history of working-class struggles for basic human rights and justice is often lost in American educational textbooks. But the connection is strong between such workers' movements and the ethics of social responsibility.

Labor movement leaders in the past such as Fannie Lou Hamer, Walter Reuther, and Cesar Chavez, with strong support from their rank and file, have pushed for changes in public policies to benefit all working Americans. These policies have ranged from groundbreaking occupational health and safety laws to the establishment of fair wages. As labor and spiritual leader A. J. Muste remarked as he strove in the 1960s to connect the struggle for economic justice with civil rights' marches, "I have learned to pray with my feet."

Today, the labor movement faces new challenges in focusing its organizing efforts beyond bread and butter issues. Among the issues that matter to contemporary workers and link to social responsibility are paid family leave, better wages and benefits options for part-time work, and shorter and more flexible work weeks that would allow more time for family and community.

RELIGIOUS ROOTS

In religious traditions, all those who toil are seen as having the potential of serving the common good. The Judaic idea of a covenant between God and people presents a vision of a community where communal responsibility connects all members. Individual fulfillment and closeness to God are dependent upon fulfillment of the needs of the community. As theologian Martin Buber states, "Whoever is full of himself has no room for God."[13]

In the Talmudic Jewish tradition, work is seen as central to fulfilling the creation story. God began the story of creation, and the role of human beings is to continue the creation. Human beings have a choice of whether to do work that cultivates the world, meyashvei olam, or work that destroys the world, mevalei olam.[14] Work that is constructive, that cultivates, is a moral good. For the ancient sages, such work was sacred whether one was a tiller of the soil or a scholar.

A. D. Gordon provided a pragmatic philosophy for the modern Israeli kibbutz movement by uniting the tiller of the soil with the mindful scholar.[15] For Gordon, authentic work is labor that builds society. Other forms of work are mere busywork, the mere relentless doing of tasks. Such work causes alienation for workers and serves only superficial purposes. Both manual labor and intellectual labor can serve the community and thus lead the individual to help redeem the world. Doing such work was the way an individual could "heal the heart" and, through such healing, the nation and then the world could be healed as well.

It is noteworthy that, even according to orthodox Jewish teaching, doing healing work is permitted on the Sabbath. While almost all forms of work are forbidden on the rest day, the Talmud states it is permissible to transact work that has to do with saving a life. According to this view, when some of the biotech employees rushed back from their vacations to grow necessary cell cultures for a burn victim, they were doing sacred work. It mirrors what the biotech employees themselves expressed as the deep meaning that their work provides.

The power of doing good work also has been a recurrent theme in Catholic teaching. Through the Vatican, the Catholic Church in 1891 began its modern social and economic analysis with the publication of *Rerum Novarum* or *On the Conditions of the Working Classes*. Pope Leo XIII was responding to the massive upheavals caused by the Industrial Revolution. The major issues were similar to those faced by the Church today: dwindling participation, social apathy, and the growth of materialism.[16] Many church leaders over a century ago understood that based on its own ethical traditions, the Church needed to address core values about work in the new economic order.

Pope Leo rejected the notion that labor was only a commodity to be bought and sold in the market. He established the Church's belief in the interdependence of labor and capital since "each needs the other." Further stating that government had a proper role in redistributing wealth, Pope Leo also legitimized the rights of workers to join and form workers' associations and unions to protect themselves. In 1981, John Paul II affirmed these rights in *Laborum Exercens* in which he stated, "human work is a key, probably the essential key, to the whole social question."

In 1986, the United States Catholic bishops issued *Economic Justice for All,* a pastoral letter on Catholic social teaching and the economy. The purpose of the letter was to call Catholics "to use the resources of our faith, the strength of our economy, and the opportunities of our democracy to shape a society that better protects the dignity and basic rights of our sisters and brothers, both in this land and around the world."[17] And the letter makes clear that access to employment must be open to all without discrimination: the healthy and disabled, natives and immigrants.

The pastoral letter raises the question of whether economic life enhances or threatens our life together as a community. Flowing from the doctrine that the person is sacred, the clearest reflection of God among us, the letter states that every economic decision must be judged in light of whether it protects or undermines individual dignity. And because human dignity "can be realized and protected only in community," there is an obligation to have economic institutions serve the common good.

While defending private ownership as contributing to creativity and initiative, the letter states that Catholic teaching insists that accumulation of wealth be limited by the demands of the common good. As Pope Paul VI taught, "No one is justified in keeping for exclusive use what they don't need when others lack necessities."[18] The letter is clear that the Church opposes both collectivist approaches to the economy and the unimpeded market.

In calling for a "new American experiment," the Catholic bishops recall the Gospels and the special obligation to the poor.

They restate the teaching of Christ that the justice of a society is tested by the treatment of the poor. The covenant with Israel was measured by how the poor were treated. In Proverbs we saw how the Woman of Valor was honored for stretching out her hands to the poor. Therefore, the bishops see an interactive association between a good society and empowering the poor. Powerlessness of the poor wounds the whole community. Decreasing inequity raises up both the poor and everyone in the society. A "new American experiment" in economic rights would create an order that guarantees the conditions for human dignity in the economic sphere for every person.

Finally, the letter reaffirms the Church's concern for family life by asking that socioeconomic policies and work organizations be evaluated by their impact on family well-being. Businesses are seen as needing new patterns of organization that would be more supportive of family life. Such change would benefit both the business goals of employers and the needs of employees and their families.

Protestant denominations have had many voices on the issue of work and social responsibility. The Episcopal *Book of Common Prayer* reflects a sense of calling rather than simply the notion of career as shaping human work endeavors. Its prayer for Labor Day says, "So guide us in the work we do, that we may do it not for the self alone, but for the common good."

A sense of calling was very much part of the early Protestant Reformation doctrine that linked doing good work by the individual to serving the public world and, in that labor, serving God. This Protestant tradition influenced the founding fathers and their beliefs about the deep connection between work, the common good, and a moral life. The Reformers were united in their belief that the primary purpose of work was to serve God and benefit society. People who pursued work and wealth only to satisfy personal interests were denounced. Work was to be done within an ethic of grace, an ethic that shunned the notion of the self-made person.[19]

Since their early teachings, various Protestant denominations have set forth declarations that connect work with social responsibility. In 1986, the American Baptist Churches issued a resolution that stated, "industry is a social service whose ruling motive should be not the profit of the few, but the welfare of all, and that the service motive must become the dominant spirit in both the methods and processes of industry."

Similarly, the United Methodist Church in its 1996 Book of Discipline declared, "we believe in the right and duty of persons to work for the glory of God and the good of themselves and others . . . and in the elimination of economic and social distress." And, as a final example of current Protestant thinking, the 1999 Social Statement of the Evangelical Lutheran Church in America professed, "as stewards of what God has entrusted to us, we should use available resources to generate jobs for livelihood of more people . . . wealth should serve or benefit others so that they also might live productively."

In the twentieth century, Martin Luther King, Jr., perhaps best represents that integration of Protestant Christian ideals of a "calling" with the Jeffersonian republican ideals of building a just nation. He affirms the prophetic themes of raising up the poor and honoring the tillers of the land with the democratic principle of all members of society enjoying the fruits of liberty. King's strong adherence to nonviolence also had roots in the Quaker and Mennonite religious traditions, which in the 1800s guided many to join antislavery and social change movements.

In his last years, King increasingly targeted his nonviolent actions on issues of worker rights and economic justice. In his last 1967 Presidential Address to the Southern Christian Leadership Conference, he spoke of the challenge for African Americans to organize their economic as well as political power. He urged the development through nonviolent action of programs that would insure a guaranteed annual income, full employment, and "new forms of work that enhance the social good."[20] King went on to provide an eloquent formula for the connection between work and a good society: "The fact is that work which improves the condition of mankind, the work which extends knowledge and increases power and enriches literature and elevates thought, is not done to secure a living. It is not the work of slaves driven to their tasks either by the task, by the taskmaster, or by animal necessity. It is the work of men who somehow find a form of work that brings a security for its own sake and a state of society where want is abolished."[21]

In addition to the Jewish and Christian traditions, other religions also have precepts that connect beliefs to social responsibility. One of the most important principles of Islam, for example, is that all things belong to God and that wealth is thus held by human beings in trust. A major goal of Islam is to provide human beings with a practical system for living so the trust can be fulfilled. Universal rights of humanity are to be observed and respected under all circumstances. The teachings of Islam concerning social responsibilities are based on kindness and consideration for others. The Prophet says one cannot be a good Muslim, a person who responds to the call of Islam, unless one practices such principles. "And know that whatever thing you gain, a fifth of it is for Allah and for the Apostle and for the near of kin and the orphans and the needy and the wayfarer, if you believe in Allah and in that which We revealed to Our servant, on the day of distinction, the day on which the two parties met; and Allah has power over all things."[22]

Buddhism is primarily concerned with individual enlightenment as set forth through the Four Noble Truths and the Eightfold Path. The social responsibility that springs from these teachings comes from the strong belief in doing no harm. The reduction of suffering in the world—for all living things—marks the journey of a good life.[23]

A final example of nonwestern practices that link social responsibility and work is the Korean system of *kyeh*.[24] In this system a group of people pools their money together, draws lots, and then gives the winner the pooled resources with which they can start a business or build some sort of livelihood. The group continues to meet and pool resources until everyone has become a winner! In immigrant Korean communities, the *kyeh* system helped launch many neighborhood enterprises, so that loans were not needed from high-interest banks. The emphasis on community and the common good is a central feature of the *kyeh* system, which has its counterpart in many other immigrant societies.

Both secular and religious frameworks support the idea that social responsibility, a connection to a sense of community at work, is crucial for having dignity at work. How, then, is it realized: Are there different paths to social responsibility depending on the work you do? Do younger workers care about this at all? Do new forms of work enhance or impede opportunities for attaining this element of dignity?

DIFFERENT JOBS, DIFFERENT PATHWAYS

Manufacturing

It was a hot day in Boston's Chinatown. We sat in a small office and could smell the pungent odor of the restaurant downstairs. Eight women, all in their fifties and sixties, all originally immigrants from China were gathered there to share their story of "doing good work."[25]

These women were garment workers, stitching blouses and shirts together for various manufacturers in the Northeast. They always had worked with their hands, but their minds and hearts also went into their stitches: "I sewed collars into shirts for eighteen years—there is no one on earth who can put a collar in better. I am a collar artist!" Some women did collars and others stitched sleeves or were artists of buttons and buttonholes. Their pride in their skill showed in their faces and filled up the room. In the manual labor process, dignity in work partly comes from producing something of beauty, in terms of efficiency and elegance, even if it is produced on an assembly line. The pride in producing a product that is valued by others in the community for its fine craftsmanship is experienced as a contribution to the common good. Economist Thorsten Veblen called the instinct for workmanship one of the deep strengths of the American character, which, if weakened, would undermine our society.[26]

But more than pride in the well-stitched collar or cuff was the conviction that their labors were of social value: "There are three things that each person needs—food, house, clothing—and we take care of one of these. The clothes we do are everywhere, keeping the children, the grown men and women, warm and well." Though the clothes the women made were shipped to markets and stores across the nation, the women seemed to picture actual people wearing the blouses and shirts that came out of their factory. They wanted to be sure that they did the best job possible since they were "clothing the world out there."

The women did not minimize the hardness of the workdays, often lengthened by mandated overtime to meet seasonal production demands. Their unionized wages were decent but modest, and the factory, your basic noisy, stuffy environment. However, the women had each other and had a collective sense of being joined to their adopted country through their work. They experienced themselves as socially responsible workers and as good citizens of America.

The Singer Sewing Machine plant had been located in Elizabeth, New Jersey, for more than 100 years and was the flagship of the Singer Corporation, a major multinational in the mid-twentieth century. Anthropologist Katherine Newman studied the lives and fortunes of workers in the plant during the 1980s.[27] She found that for decades, the flagship plant, applauded as the most innovative factory in the United States, had also been the heart of the town. Like the old textile mills in New England, the company built the town and provided livelihoods for generations of its citizens. The recreation fields were built by the firm; the softball teams were fielded by the firm; and you were buried in the firm's cemetery. Even the mayor of the town came from the factory's shop floor.

The manufacturing workers employed in the firm were proud of the work they did. This pride rested on three factors. First, the workers were skilled craftsmen and upheld a tradition of building a fine product. Singer sewing machines were notable for both the efficiency of their parts and for their beauty. They were elegant machines, hand decorated with gold filigree.

Second, the manufacturing workers felt pride in contributing to the nation's war efforts. During World War I, World War II, and the Korean War, the Singer factory, along with many others across America, had been converted to support the war effort: instead of sewing machines the workers produced ammunitions. Their work was seen by others as well as themselves as very important to the nation's defense. This became part of the dignity at work that was passed down from one generation in the plant to another. The notion that "we were part of the war victory" was a narrative that linked the individual daily tasks in the plant to the fulfillment of national social responsibility.

Third, the individual manufacturing workers at the Singer plant experienced the rise and eventual fall of the plant as part of a community. For years the workers had thought of their work as part of the larger whole—the whole being first the workers in the plant, then the whole of all the families connected to the plant, then the whole of the community, and, finally, the whole of the nation. The connection between the self and the larger wholes was real, not an abstraction. This connection was reversed when outsiders, who had no connection to the town or plant, came in during the 1970s and began to divest the plant's resources. The unthinkable happened when Singer stopped manufacturing sewing machines. Workers had been bound to a larger community that was being eliminated, and individuals were left to cope alone. As individuals, they did not know how to rescue themselves. When the factory closed, generations of dignity at work were buried as well.

Service Sector

Home health care workers, representing the millions of Americans employed today in the service sector, travel a different road in fulfilling the value of social responsibility on the job.[28] Their craftsmanship is of a different sort than the garment workers or the machinists but just as key to their maintenance of dignity at work. For home health employees, the craft of their work is centered on preserving the integrity of the person in their care. The mark of good work is more difficult to measure than the products of the manufacturing sector but just as real: the ability to cheer someone, to alter a patient's mood for the better, to reconcile family members in the face of illness and aging.

In fact, the very essence of care-giving work is its relational quality. The patient or client is the barometer of doing a good job. The attributes necessary for doing a good job—building a sense of trust and reciprocal respect—are the same qualities that are important in sustaining local communities and the nation. Care-giving work thus contributes to what researchers call social capital—the mutual aid necessary to hold a society together rather than let it unravel into a set of isolated individuals. The work that home health workers do is twofold: In itself it enacts socially responsibility *and* it builds socially responsible values for the larger society.

However, political scientist Deborah Stone has discussed how once home health care work was taken over by bureaucratic organizations, norms of productivity and efficiency replaced relational caring as the goal. "The goals of organizational survival, of balancing the books and lowering costs, displace the goals of making someone feel cared for and improving someone's health."[29] Even though research has documented that relational caring has measurable positive effects on physical and mental health outcomes, the short-term task costs are what counts in the formal system.

Many health care workers, like other service sector workers, continue to strive to be socially responsible in their jobs in an informal way. For example, after Medicare cutbacks forced many long-term clients to have a reduction of home care services, care providers often felt the new insurance rules violated their own sense of decency. So they would stop by on their own time after work or on days off. "You'd stop by to check on a neighbor or a friend. Why wouldn't you do it just because they're a client?" said one care provider.[30] This form of resistance to bureaucratic rules has allowed health care workers a pathway to continue their jobs without forfeiting their sense of social responsibility. In most cases this is happening not as part of their official jobs but in spite of the new organizational forms of health care in America.

Even doctors, who are on the highest rungs of the service sector and health provider ladder, have been caught in the no-win situation of choosing between being accountable to their Hippocratic oath of caring for patients and being accountable to the bottom-line monetary goals of health maintenance organizations. Medicine has long been viewed as the ultimate socially responsive profession. Many minority students especially choose to enter its ranks precisely because they wish to give something back to their communities.[31] Practicing medicine has been the ultimate career—for financial rewards, status, and for making a difference. The changing culture of health care in America, however, is causing many doctors to feel ethically undermined. Just as the Singer Sewing

Machine workers, they feel the door shutting on preserving dignity through their work.

❖ ❖ ❖

My mother was a school teacher for her whole working life, one of the most common service sector jobs for a woman of her generation. When my father became ill, it was her salary that kept the family afloat. She keenly felt the social responsibility that came with her job: "What could be more valuable than opening the doors for education for children?" She taught physically handicapped and emotionally disturbed children, often from poor neighborhoods, before there was Head Start or mainstreaming. The children in her classroom needed (and she felt deserved) extra understanding and caring, given the extra challenges they faced from other children and adults alike. She also knew that a hungry child could not easily keep up attention so she personally brought in breakfast for her children. She made sure they had respectable clothing and shoes, because she realized that if a child did not have decent clothes, that child felt shame and was unable to think of herself as someone of worth. In her 35 years as a special education teacher, she felt great pride in both providing a livelihood for her family and having work that made a social contribution.

Today, many teachers feel both undervalued and cut off from the support of the communities they wish to serve. In a California study of pay equity, it was found that parking lot attendants who watched over cars made more per hour than child care teachers watching over preschoolers.[32] Teachers are blamed for a variety of ills from poor test scores in communities where parents are barely involved with their kids' education to violence in the schools in a society where guns are easily bought and media images celebrate violent behavior.

❖ ❖ ❖

Service sector workers confront a paradox: While their jobs are indeed serving—providing a socially useful function for others— their jobs, even if respectable, are undervalued. One explanation is the gendered nature of many service jobs, especially those involving care giving. Until recently, most care giving was done in the private sphere. Historian Stephanie Coontz provides evidence that prior to the nineteenth century, fathers and mothers were both involved in ongoing child rearing and care-giving responsibilities.[33] Because all work was domestic—done in the household—both men's and women's work was valued.

However, the preindustrial families' integration of care-giving and worker roles unraveled as paid work moved outside the home. Polarized notions of the ideal worker and ideal family care giver emerged, setting up separations between home and work. The boundary was divided by sex, with women assigned to the home and men to "bringing home the bacon." The cult of domesticity that arose in the mid-1800s produced the concept of the ideal parent and care giver as the white middle-class mother who stayed at home. Her labors were private, invisible, and not counted as part of the production process valued by the economy.[34]

Over the twentieth century, with the emergence of the dual-income family, care giving has shifted to the public sector, through profit and nonprofit corporations and agencies. Women have been the majority of paid workers in this sector, but because the roles they perform have never been perceived as valuable productive work, the jobs of serving and care giving remain financially unrewarded, and the relational character of their tasks unappreciated. So the very jobs that connect work to social responsible caring for others—through health, education, and other services—remain on the bottom of the success ladder.

Information and High Tech

In 1981 there was an air controllers strike that riveted the nation. President Ronald Reagan fired all the controllers who were members of the Patco union striking for better hours and compensation. During the election, this union had broken ranks with the labor movements' endorsement of the Democrat's presidential candidate; Reagan was firing the only organized labor union that had backed him.

The air traffic controllers were primarily men of working-class origins who came to their jobs via the military, where they had been given the high level of skill training necessary to perform the demanding technical work.[35] Many had volunteered for military service during the Vietnam War, and they took their extremely skilled work very seriously.

Their high-tech work was also very stressful. Their jobs were organized around rolling eight-hour shifts: on eight hours, off eight hours, on eight hours again. It made for constant fatigue. You neither got to know your colleagues well nor was any friend in another occupation on your schedule, which made the work isolating as well as physically stressful. And to do their job, controllers had to be constantly part of an intense communication system, bound by radio contact covering an extensive area, wearing headphones all shift long. To be a controller meant you were an information tech survivor; first surviving the intensive boot camp training that flunks over half of those who start, then surviving the everyday intensive high-tech demands of your job.

But during the strike the air traffic controllers, while losing their livelihood, held onto their sense of dignity about their work. They saw themselves as upholding the public's safety. They sacrificed each day for the sake of others in the nation, just as they had done during the war. Their information sector jobs were crucial to national security and to the personal well-being of millions of Americans who took to the friendly skies. They felt their jobs were noble. This sensibility helped them to retain a sense of dignity in the face of assaults on their financial security.

In fact, when the Reagan administration blacklisted the controllers, letting nearby military contractors know that if they hired any strikers they would lose contract renewals, the controllers' sense that they were in the right only increased. They were a union of brave men, in the tradition of the pioneers on the frontier, taking personal risks in order to provide a safe haven for others in the nation.

Biotech employees are another group of high-tech pioneers.[36] Their work is on the cutting edge of discovery for new drugs and biological advances. Biotechnology, in the broadest sense, is a series of techniques used to manipulate living organisms to provide useful processes and products. The industry was born in the 1970s, when millions of dollars in venture capital flowed into small companies focused on complex diseases such as AIDS, cancer, and Alzheimer's. Employees include highly trained scientists and technicians who daily set out to bring therapies and cures to a waiting public. A passion for making a difference drives most biotech employees.

The work of biotech employees has a valued meaning outside of the workplace. Workers express that their families understand their commitment to do good work even when it interferes with family activities. One research technician gave an example of work as an expression of values of social meaning beyond the lab: "It was summer and we had just arrived in Maine for a week of family vacation. On the radio we heard a news report about a child accident victim, and I realized that the cell replacement therapy we were working on would maybe be called for in the medical response. So I called the company and, sure enough, I was asked to come in. I drove back, worked over Saturday and Sunday helping to begin the cell culture, and then drove back. My family knew I needed to do that to enjoy the rest of the vacation."

The strong sense of serving the public good helps biotech employees deal with the ever-present uncertainties of working in a fluid industry where firm life can be very short. Just as the controllers offset their job stress with a commitment to public safety, biotech people balance their economic insecurity with a commitment to prevent and cure diseases. Both groups of knowledge workers in our new economy integrate their work selves with their values about social responsibility. While they are in important ways risk takers, they avoid the dangers of segregating their lives at work from their lives as family members, neighbors, and citizens.[37]

For workers in manufacturing, in the service sector, and in the information and high-tech sector, there are different paths to connect their daily labors to values of social responsibility. In a variety of ways, workers experience this connection. However, there are many employees whose workplaces interfere with making such a connection. They exist across all sectors of the economy, often wondering if or how they can feel a sense of value about their work. They work outside an economic framework that fosters achievement of a social good.

By the 1990s, most people in the labor force were struggling to juggle responsibilities at home with responsibilities at work, and engagement with the larger community became even tougher. The difficulty of keeping up a commitment to community associations has occurred on top of the difficult search for dignity at the workplace. The culture of work itself makes it hard to resolve both these difficulties.

SEARCHING FOR COMMUNITY TIME

In the late 1990s, a heated debate broke out among researchers on the question of whether Americans were keeping up their civic involvement. In our earlier discussion of the historical roots of the value of social responsibility, we heard loud and clear from French observer Alexis de Tocqueville and our own Thomas Jefferson that American democracy depends upon civic participation. If it is true that Americans no longer give at home or in the office, then the fabric of our democratic society may be irretrievably unraveling! But is it true? The short answer is, it depends. It depends on how we define community participation and who is responding to the question.[38]

Robert Putnam's book *Bowling Alone* struck a nerve by asserting that more Americans were now bowling by themselves rather than in leagues, and this represented an overall decline in traditional civic engagement in our nation. He went on to cite diminished participation in many civic groups, such as the PTA and the civic organizations like the Lions and Elks. Politicians used his research to lament the decline in American social capital and to call for a renewal of voluntarism and communal efforts.

But other researchers find a different story. Everett Carll Ladd, director of the Roper Center, debunks the idea that America is becoming a nation of loners. Membership, according to Ladd, is shifting from established older groups to new ones. For example, kids soccer has become a new locus of parental involvement, and environmental affiliations have replaced fraternal organizations.

Some suggest the issue is not the dissolution of civic participation but the change in its form. Robert Wuthnow thinks that though Americans are turning away from large bureaucratic organizations like the Red Cross, they're instead joining smaller, more loosely structured associations. Fitting the favored, flexible lifestyle for the twenty-first century, "people can move in and out of issues and organizations." This fluidity better fits the ad hoc nature of modern life with sporadic associations in place of longer term memberships.

Theda Skocpol argues that many of our national volunteer organizations were never simple local community associations. Such groups as the Red Cross, the Salvation Army, and the American

Legion worked closely with the government to address social justice issues. The American Legion lobbied for the GI Bill, and the precursor to the PTA, the National Congress of Mothers, pressed for laws for women's pensions. Skocpol asserts, "Organized civil society in the United States has never flourished apart from active government." The increasing public disenchantment with the federal government especially may thus impede the traditional associations of the past. And Skocpol believes that the new, smaller sporadic groups are not worthy substitutes because they fail to engage individuals with the larger community and with important national policy issues.

Francis Fukuyama, while suggesting that the "rights genera-tion" of the 1970s and 1980s substituted me for we, offers an optimistic view that replenishment of social capital will occur. He bases his optimism on sociobiological research that contends that humans seek cooperation and connection. Thus, while renewal of civic participation is not easy, it will bloom given the "very powerful innate human capacity for reconstituting social order." The ques-tion he does not answer is if and how institutions that shape human existence, such as corporations, will transform their bottom-line, market-driven cultures.

❖   ❖   ❖

Back at the ranch house, most workers in America are hard pressed to find the time to participate in any sustained way. Sporadic associations do not seem to be equal substitutes in shoring up a large sense of we. One bank manager, looking weary at the end of a ten-hour workday, mourned his lost involvement with the Shriners and his volunteer activities with burn victims. He expressed the dual dilemma faced by others: At work, he does not feel connected to the larger community and does not view his job as data manager as having social relevance. His community connection used to come from time spent outside of work in civic involvement. But more and more, he is working longer and longer hours which prohibit such involvement. He has no way of winning back his connection unless something changes.

In the next chapters, we turn to the tales of two workplaces attempting to make positive changes. At these workplaces, employees each day face the bottom-line culture of corporate America. Employees in the biotech industry, confident that their work is socially responsive, struggle with concerns for job security and family responsibilities. Employees in a bank firm begin a bold experiment: They will try to change their work organization to meet profit goals *and* family and community commitments. Their experiment is aimed at achieving this win-win agenda.

These two industries—banking and biotechnology—are representative of many of the changing workplaces in our nation. Banking is increasingly a place where there are large-scale mergers and acquisitions, where values of tradition, local ties, and employer-employee loyalty have been replaced by e-commerce, global finance, and fluidity. Old occupations such as bank teller are disappearing as new computer-based jobs emerge. Like bank employees, many Americans find themselves working in the midst of reorganization and structured change.

Biotech is made up of small to medium firms, typical of the size of firms where most Americans work. Biotech workers are considered knowledge workers, in an industry that, unlike banking, did not even exist fifty years ago. Younger workers in particular find themselves in similar new industries, in newly emerging occupations. Keeping up with technological change and knowledge breakthroughs is the name of the game for many of us.

The employment picture in banking and biotech also reflects the increasing numbers of women and minorities in the American labor force in general. For example, minorities now constitute 22 percent of jobs in banking while women make up nearly 50 percent of biotech workers. These two industries, therefore, provide representative portraits of existing workplaces in America. The tales of two workplaces will give us a closer look at how the search for dignity plays out in the real world of work.

Present

The Biotech Story
Walking on Jell-O

When the biotech industry burst on the scene in the 1970s, it was seen as a network of sexy start-up companies resting on the shaky foundation of venture capital. The firms tended to be small, with more than half employing fewer than 50 employees and 90 percent employing fewer than 500. In this "small but beautiful" environment, some of the most research-intensive work ever done by humans has been conducted. Just in the United States in one year, 1999, the biotech industry spent almost $11 billion on research and development. This money produced about 153,000 jobs in over 1,200 companies clustered in a few national regions—metropolitan Boston, Silicon Valley, Texas, and North Carolina's Triangle area.

By 1996, in metro Boston alone about 150 biotech firms existed. It made sense for the firms to be there. Boston is known for its highly educated and skilled workforce, and its proximity to some of the nation's finest universities and research institutes has been a big plus. The research of biotech firms often grew out of ideas generated from inside these ivy towers. It was also not unusual for folks who once donned lab coats to switch to business suits to head the biotech entrepreneurial enterprises.

Lots of money has been made or lost in the industry. Start-ups tend to be privately held firms, with less than one-third of the companies publicly traded. The nature of the work itself is sexy— applying state-of-the-art biological advances to new forms of drugs and to remedies for some of the most challenging human diseases—AIDS, arthritis, cancer, and Alzheimer's. At the same time, the chances of any one new product ever making it to market are extraordinary.

The product development cycle is uniquely long, taking 7 to 12 *years* to move from the initial scientific idea to an approved market product. The process is extremely slow, compared to other knowledge-based industries such as computer software. This reflects the flow from scientific experimentation, unpredictable trials, passing a stiff regulatory review process, and then facing possible marketing issues from doctors, insurance companies, and governments here and abroad. It is estimated that of every 500 new ideas initially pursued only 1 ever gets to a shelf in the marketplace.

So the everyday labors of the biotech industry offer no sure guarantees of success and, in fact, more often produce tales of failure. It is a risky business. But because of the very uncertainties of the biotech industry, it can be viewed as a harbinger of the future professional workplace in our nation.

For the future workplace, the name of the game is change. Employers and employees will need to find new ways to manage the changes that come from transforming market demands, tech-nologies, newer forms of communications and knowledge exchange, environmental conditions, and governmental regula-tions. They also will need to navigate new contractual arrangements to cover the changes in time and space of the new ways of working— flex time and virtual time; on site and off site; as standard employees and as contingency workers. Biotechnology, though a small industry, reflects patterns of working under conditions of change that will become more common in the years ahead.

The biotech industry employs knowledge workers with professional degrees and technical skills; its small firms are devoutly entrepreneurial and heavily networked with other firms and institutions; and its reliance on borrowed money and the vicissitudes of clinical trials generate a climate of uncertainty for the biotech firm and for the biotech employee.

Thus, when the Radcliffe Public Policy Center became interested in understanding how workers in America today dealt with the new economic conditions expected in the years ahead, the biotech industry offered an ideal place to explore.[1] How do employees in a work environment that offers the opportunity to be information and high-tech sector leaders but little long-range security respond day to day? What do their lives look like in terms of time for family and community? And, have they composed a work life that offers the dignity that comes from achieving a livelihood, self-respect, and social responsibility?

GETTING INTO THE FIELD

Doing fieldwork is an intense and often unpredictable science. The first job was to assemble an interdisciplinary research team who had complementary areas of knowledge necessary to explore the questions at hand. The primary team included an organizational theorist, two anthropologists, an economist, a labor and industrial researcher, and a sociologist. We enjoyed considerable research assistance from a terrific group of graduate and undergraduate students from a variety of disciplines and schools.

The next job was to secure ample funding to cover the costs of being in the field for two years. The Alfred P. Sloan Foundation had an emerging interest in work-family issues, and we were fortunate to be among their first grantees in this research area.

And then, there was the challenge of the sites themselves. We had already made the decision to stay within one geographic region so we could investigate the relationship among regional economic conditions, work processes at each site, and how employees constructed their daily work, family, and community lives. Massachusetts, a leading biotech region, made logistic sense given our familiarity and closeness to the area. Collaboration was also possible with the Massachusetts Biotechnology Council (MBC), which was willing to help distribute a survey to its list of 113 local biotech firms. This 1998 survey was used to give us a representative profile of companies in the region, providing a larger picture before we selected three sites for more intense study.

From the survey, we uncovered the following portrait of biotech firms in Massachusetts. The biotech workforce is composed of highly educated workers—85 percent have a bachelor's degree; 25 percent have a Ph.D.; about half (46 percent) are women; about half (46 percent) have children.

Seventy-five percent of the companies have less than 150 employees, with 45 percent having less than 50. Like most American workers, biotech employees tend to work in small- to medium-size firms.

In terms of occupations, 49 percent of employees were researchers, 19 percent were administrators, 12 percent were in manufacturing, and smaller groupings were in regulatory or marketing and sales positions. Generally, workers had a low job tenure, on average holding their jobs for three years. For Americans in general the average is six years.

The national economic forces of layoffs and restructuring were felt by the biotech firms. One out of four firms experienced layoffs during the 1995-97 period. Human Resources personnel reported that the uncertainty of business outcomes was a source of morale problems for their firm.

For those retaining their jobs, the hours were often longer than the companies' official full-time workweek: More than three-fourths of managers and staff work greater than the official workweek. Only 5 percent report working part-time.

Most firms reported some existing work-family policies, including family leave (91 percent); personal sick days (88 percent); and leave to care for sick relatives (75 percent). However, only 3 percent offered on-site child care options and only 7 percent had programs that allowed workers to take time for community service. Indeed, this lack of private sector response to the multiple roles employees have in their daily lives is true across industries and regions in America. And, this lack of private sector response mirrors the lack of public policy initiatives. As a nation we lag behind all other advanced industrialized countries in providing access to child care and *paid* family leave.

SITE SELECTION

We had a number of criteria in mind when we thought about selecting three firms for the case studies. Because of the great volatility in the industry, some firms lasted only a short time or existed only on paper. We needed firms that had some history, that had at least a shot at being around for the two years we would undertake the study. We therefore looked for firms with a track record of having made it through at least one clinical trial in the past and not a "virtual" company with no current products and no products in sight.

Key and highly important to the selection process was the openness of the CEOs and leading managers to the study. The study design included many hours of interviews for managers, administrators, and employees, which translated into time and effort on behalf of the research. And, ahead of time we could only outline in the broadest possible way when, how, and who we would be meeting with over the two years. The beauty and the challenge of qualitative fieldwork is refining questions as you get more deeply involved in the study and being creative with your design so that you can optimize the learning process. This meant a certain leap of faith for the CEOs and other firm leaders. They needed to think the goals of the study were sufficiently worthwhile to open their doors and cooperate. In some sense, only firms whose leadership cared about work, family, and community issues or were at least curious about such issues, would welcome us into their workplaces and lives.[2]

A final criterion was the size of the firm. We knew one of the contributions of our study would be to turn the work-family-community lens on smaller companies. But if a company was too small—under 30 people—it would not have the range of personnel necessary for us to get a full picture of work processes in the biotech industry. Also, since we wished to gain access to human resource data—such as turnover rates, morale issues, company work-family-community policies—only firms large enough to sustain an HR office made sense.

With those criteria in mind, the senior researchers for the study reviewed a listing of possible sites, did some further background gathering of information, and then made a short list of half a dozen firms. Personal conversations were set up at the possible sites with a number of CEOs. By the end of the three-month preparation stage, two firms had come on board. Two months later, a third company said yes. By the start of 1998 we were ready to enter the field in earnest. In the following descriptions of the three selected firms, the pseudonyms given during the study are used.

Prima was founded in the first wave of biotech companies. Like many other early companies, it began with a business strategy that focused on becoming a large, if not fully integrated, biopharmaceutical company. To this end, Prima built a respectable "product pipeline," achieved some success, and grew to a medium-sized company. It did not, however, develop a solid revenue base and thus restructured in the mid-1990s. These changes included one large layoff. The company at the start of fieldwork was less than half of its peak size. Prima's business strategy has concentrated resources on research and development (R&D) and building alliances. It has been in a somewhat precarious position because of its reliance on financing from partners, a situation faced by many biotech firms. Even when its situation improved via a multimillion dollar alliance with a larger company, it remained in an uncertainty spiral which shapes life in the firm.

Segunda was founded in the early 1980s and also began with a vision of becoming a fully integrated pharmaceutical company. It achieved FDA approval of its lead product and has maintained a production facility on site. Segunda has licensed its proprietary products to several corporate partners and actively seeks collaborations with academic institutions and industry. It has a modest income stream that creates internal and external optimism about longer-term chances for success. Even so, it has suffered some setbacks and restructuring. Its ultimate success is dependent on products currently in the pipeline, because a biotech firm needs more than one product to be viable. The atmosphere at Segunda is conservatively hopeful.

Tertia is the largest and most developed of the three sites. Founded in the late 1980s as a small company that developed cutting-edge technology in medical therapeutics, it became a subsidiary of a large, financially secure company in the 1990s. This position provides it with steady access to significant financial and intellectual resources. Tertia's lead product has received FDA approval. The site is now focused on increasing its manufacturing and sales capabilities, some of which are managed by its parent company. In its manufacturing unit, some employees were switched to a four-day workweek to accommodate production demands. The company as a whole has relative security, especially within the biotech community, but has not yet achieved long-lasting success. Much depends on its marketing success with those outside the firm—key doctor networks, health insurance companies—and ongoing clinical trials.

For all of the sites, change was ongoing during the fieldwork period. Prima merged with another company, Segunda relocated and Tertia's product market expanded.[3] Employees at all three experienced layoffs and attrition. Surrounded by all the dynamic fluctuations, we were questioning people about the nature of their work, how they managed to have a life, and what provided a sense of meaning and security amidst it all.

LIVELIHOOD

Biotech employees hold jobs that are the "good jobs" in a global economy that rewards knowledge and high-tech skills. All but the lower clerical positions allow employees to secure middle-class incomes, and the more senior scientists and managers, through a combination of salary and stock options, can do very well.

Most biotech workers live in suburbia, with salaries ranging from mid-$40,000 to $100,000 for Ph.D.-level employees, and from $20,000 to $40,000 for employees with B.A.s. Those with high school or technical degrees earn between $15,000 and $30,000. More than 80 percent of the biotech employees are home owners.

Despite the seemingly endless insecurity of biotech firms, the employees themselves often see themselves quite grounded in their work. This paradox is explained by their strong attachment to scientific discovery, their fellow colleagues, and their own careers. Each plays a role in allowing the biotech worker not only a way to gain a livelihood but a way to experience a sense of larger reward and opportunity.

Many scientists like Georgia at Segunda came to biotech as an escape from a position in an academic institution. From an early age

Georgia knew she loved biology. Being female, she was originally pushed into a pre-med track, the pathway deemed appropriate for a girl who liked science. But Georgia soon discovered that her real passion was research, and she was skilled at working with her hands in the lab. A college teacher became a mentor and encouraged her to pursue a biochem degree. By the time she was a post doc, she thought she was on her way to a tenured job in a good academic setting.

Academic science, however, had gotten tougher and tougher in terms of gaining tenure, and this was especially true for women. Academic scientists are often required to raise their own research funds. The pace is grueling, with scientists putting in 60, 70, and sometimes 80 hours a week. Being wedded to science has been viewed as the only way to be taken seriously by many in the academic community. So Georgia, seeing the writing on the wall and feeling her chances to succeed were slim, decided to make the move: "Biotech offered me a place to make a good living, stay connected to the science I loved, and gave me a chance to move up and still have time for other things in my life."

During fieldwork, we found that the combination of good compensation and potential for promotion while being a part of a scientific enterprise was very effective in pulling people into biotech. A young man just finishing his post doc concluded, "Going into academia was not a viable choice . . . You have to bring in grant money, teach, advise, get a lab up and going. You have to put a huge amount of effort in, with little return. In biotech, they seem to compensate well and do some neat things."

Non-Ph.D. employees also felt this way. For those very interested in science careers but unable or unwilling to go the doctorate route, biotech has opened a way to succeed that's not available in the more traditional academic setting. Though Ph.D. scientists begin at higher rates of pay, employees with bachelor's or master's degrees who perform well over the years can attain the grade of scientist in biotech. This has positive, important results for personal livelihood and promotion goals. One non-Ph.D. scientist at Prima who is now a manager commented, "There had been layoffs in my former (non biotech) job and I wanted a company with decent finances . . . Money was tight and the health insurance here was better."

Over half of all the scientists interviewed mentioned the chance for advancement and promotion as the prime reason they stayed in biotech. For many this meant not just inching up a narrow internal ladder, but having an opportunity to use new skills and expand into management. One middle-aged financial officer at Segunda spoke of why he left his position in the banking industry to come to biotech: "I know everyone thinks that banking is a steady, staid place, but everything there has gotten shaky. Consolidation is the name of the game, and there is no stability. When I came to biotech, I could make a decent living and also feel that my skills were appreciated while I was learning new things . . . there is a future in combining science know-how with business know-how."

Even though biotech is largely composed of younger workers in the 25 to 40 age category, older workers who transfer in also seem attracted by the issues of livelihood, advancement, and making it in a science context. The job in biotech gave the financial officer an experience of personal mastery and an opportunity for continued growth. His words remind us that mastery and growth are important for overall job satisfaction.

THE HOPSCOTCH PROFESSIONAL

The employee's attachment to biotech, however, is not necessarily to the firm. About half of the study's respondents spoke in terms of the work of science itself and their own role as a scientist or technician. Biotech workers see themselves as science entrepreneurs—a new hybrid of worker who is neither self-employed nor a "company man." Their loyalty, on the one hand, is to the large goals of scientific discovery and to the specific objectives of their team's project. On the other hand, their loyalty is to their career. They see themselves as members of a network of professionals who can move their skills from firm to firm—a form of hopscotch. The hopscotch professional is a symbol of our new global economy.

The story of livelihood and job security is still being composed by biotech workers. They are writing new pages as the industry itself undergoes upheavals and structural changes. They have not totally given up belonging to a firm in the old-fashioned sense. Aspects of their contract promote some, if limited, attachment: Virtually all the employees in the biotech firms we studied have stock options and some stock, either because they were awarded options or stock at their hiring or as performance bonuses. While on paper this ties employees to the fortunes of a particular firm, in reality, the stock of the publicly traded companies almost always sells below the option price. As one employee concluded on company stocks, "They seem worthless to me."

Employees are also eligible for salary adjustments on a yearly basis, usually in January, and bonuses are authorized by the firm's board of directors. But again, this is often not enough to keep an individual at a specific firm if she gets a better offer elsewhere. And most biotech firms do not offer robust retirement plans. For example, in two of the biotech firms we studied, the companies contributed only up to 1 percent of salary toward a 401(k) option if the employee put in a full 5 percent. This has a long-range impact, with those who can afford to contributing the maximum allowed to their company's 401(k) plans and leaving others fully vulnerable about future security.

The nature of the work process provides an incentive for employees to stay at a specific firm. Work is primarily organized on a project level, with a group-oriented team approach. A spirit of collaboration often marks the great effort a team puts into the initiation and development of a new drug. There is a fine balance between the individual initiative and creativity necessary for scientific discovery and the teamwork needed for a project to give birth to a successful product. The overwhelming majority of surveyed biotech employees mentioned good colleagues as a strong plus at their workplace. While some scientists do become stars, most success in biotech rests on the strength of a good team. Project-based work connects individual achievement to the fortunes of the firm.

In the end, the fortunes of biotech firms—in our study Prima, Segunda, and Tertia—remain a risky business. Biotech employees deal with the "walking on Jell-O" environment by maintaining a network of contacts across firms so they can keep informed about options elsewhere—hopscotching when appropriate. The CEO of one of our sites told me, "Everyone knows everyone else in the region—so when a company is laying off or restructuring, job offers are flowing in for anyone that has a good record." Biotech workers see themselves as not necessarily at any more risk than workers in older industries such as banking and higher education. For example, they feel more on top of their destiny than most bank employees and not captured in the "publish or perish" world of academia.

Hopscotch professionals carry their occupations on their back. Their livelihood and job security is a reflection of their knowledge and their attachment to science, and, on another level, to the project at hand. This perhaps makes "walking on Jell-O" not as slippery and impossible as an outsider may think.

SELF-RESPECT

Each morning when Len gets to work at Tertia, he enters a carefully monitored changing room to get changed into the fashion of his workday: a germ-free all-white uniform that completely covers him from head to foot. He works in the quality-control unit where human cells are being grown and monitored. When he enters the room, he looks like an ordinary citizen of Massachusetts, but by the time he emerges, he resembles the media image of a man from outer space. He looks the part he is playing at his firm: a highly skilled technician whose detailed work will mean the difference between a cell culture properly calibrated and developed or a project poorly done. It is often tedious work and there are many regulations from the government and from the firm that must be meticulously followed. And, a supervisor regularly checks his work so his autonomy is limited. But he says during a focus group, "I went to a technical school to get a certificate so I could work in a science field . . . maybe I could have made more money working at another trade but I wanted work where I wouldn't be invisible."

What does Len mean by not wishing to be invisible? After all, in his white suit you can hardly tell it is him inside and even his best friend might not recognize him! But he is getting at something deeper. He wants to be doing work that is seen by others as good work, to be where doing good work is acknowledged, and to be where his own sense of worth is verified by others thinking his work is worthwhile. And according to Len, his family and friends see his work as special and valuable.

He is accountable to certain standards at work and his accountability brings him recognition from others. This connection between doing a good job and being seen and acknowledged as doing a good job dignifies the entire work environment.

BUILDING COMMUNITY AT WORK

Being a team member at his workplace, where employees count on each other's skills to get the job done, constantly connects Len to his colleagues. Len works for a firm that is known for its groundbreaking research on growing cell tissue to repair damaged human cartilage. He is part of a team that is responsible for ensuring that the process of cell growth goes smoothly and produces a high quality product. Everyone around him in the quality-control room is engaged in a task connected to the process of creating a science product of value. In some ways, the work resembles the computerized production lines at an auto plant, a division of labor, with each person at his or her station doing a particular task.

But there are major differences as well. The biotech plants are small, with most people familiar with others from all over the firm, from the CEO and the financial officer, to the range of senior and junior scientists, to the administrative and clerical workers. There is a sense of internal solidarity, even in the midst of external threat of product or market failure, that is compelling. You do not feel isolated, you are part of something larger and important. These connections make you visible to others, and they make you visible to yourself. Mutual respect is built on such connections at work.

Len speaks of his good feelings about his immediate colleagues. He notes that when he started three years earlier, people in his unit would help if problems arose. Now he in turn helps newcomers. When they began on a new product development, his supervisor provided time for more training; she never made him feel dumb even though she has a Ph.D., and he thinks she treats everyone fairly. The sense of being treated with respect and with fairness are key to his own self-respect.

Building community at work has immense value for those involved. It upholds a sense of trust and stability in a setting where change is a constant. The community building and spirit of colleagueship in biotechnology also creates a more successful culture for the firm as a whole to meet the demands of work that rely on project teams and collective brainstorming and risk taking.

This is not unlike the community trust necessary in high-risk occupations such as fire fighting, police work, and emergency room medicine.

CHANGE AGENTS

Another link that ties together biotech workers and contrasts with larger production operations is the experience of being on the cutting edge of science, of being change agents, taking risks in a community dedicated to finding cures and helpful drugs. The excitement of being part of an enterprise that celebrates scientific exploration and change is talked about in explicit ways by the employees at Prima, Segunda, and Tertia:

A Prima senior scientist observes,

Science runs on the fact that if you've got a hypothesis you try to prove it. And all of a sudden you've proved it wrong. You find some other idea. So, you can change your whole point of view . . . everything's always changing.

A Segunda data analyst says,

What I like about my work is that it's different. Week to week it changes, or month to month it changes. It's not the same old thing . . . If you're reluctant to change, biotech is not the industry for you!

And from a Tertia quality control manager,

I would say that change is what keeps me here. It's what keeps the job interesting . . . the product does change, the product line changes, and our responsibilities change . . . So there's a future involved . . . like science, you have to be flexible and adapt to change.

The culture of work in the biotech industry reflects not only an acceptance of change but a judgment that change is a good thing. Change is institutionalized in the very fabric of the work enterprise. Taking risks, making mistakes, altering course, adapting to change, and then starting over are all part of the daily life of biotech. The boredom of years at a repetitive job, common to many industries and which Adam Smith and later commentators saw as undermining human dignity, is rare in biotech. And, as change agents in biotech, individual employees experience risk taking as part of a team—they are not in the same vulnerable situations as those who are self-employed. They can have the advantage of the stimulation and opportunities that come from change and new learning that enhances self-respect, while minimizing the downside of isolated vulnerability.

In a world where change is a constant, having a work situation that creates a positive environment for change to occur is very significant for individual well-being and development. Employees can see benefits from their risk taking and share their work experiences—failures and successes—with others around them. Change is thus not an enemy but a challenge, not to be met alone but with others. The self-respect derived from doing a good job is echoed within the firm through teamwork. The dynamic quality of dignity—having internal and external contexts—is a real possibility for biotech employees.

COSTS OF CHANGE

There are things, however, that cloud an otherwise quite positive culture of respect. First, while the majority of employees seem ready to accommodate, even embrace the changes inevitable for scientific endeavors, there are moments when it has real costs as well as benefits. And the costs of change are not isolated externalities but exact their toll on individuals and on the firm.

Each of the sites we studied underwent a major change during the fieldwork, resulting in turmoil at work. At Prima, a merger caused layoffs of ten employees. Even if the majority found work by hopscotching to other firms, being laid off is not a pleasant experience and, as we have documented in earlier chapters, undermines self-respect. There is also a toll on the survivors who often miss their former colleagues, feel guilty about still being there, and in some cases, feel the extra work burdens of doing overtime to compensate for fewer employees.

At Segunda, the costs of change related to a geographic move. While the move made the commute easier for many of the senior staff, for the lower income employees who were tied to homes, child care, and other city resources near the original plant site, the move was a hardship. Some of these workers decided to change firms rather than move, again causing disruption and loss. The move itself turned out not to be as smooth as hoped for, and a year after the move, things were still not back to normal. Morale of employees was affected even among those accustomed to change.

At Tertia, when news first came of FDA approval of the new product that employees had long worked on, there was much celebration. New four-day shifts were implemented to ensure a high level of productivity. This caused disruption of work-family lives, but with input from the workers themselves and a generally upbeat atmosphere, things were moving ahead. But then there were struggles with marketing the product, and despite the change in schedule sacrifices made by employees, layoffs occurred. This was especially jolting since in the past the parent company had always absorbed redundant workers. When this safety net unexpectedly disappeared, employees were left feeling bewildered and bitter. Though the region was in the middle of a labor shortage, and most laid off workers could readily find new work, the resulting distrust and anger left scars.

The Tertia story also provides a glimpse of another complex aspect of biotech work that bears on self-respect. Biotech employees are for the most part young, married workers, half of them with children at home. Their children are also likely to be young, with 46 percent of children under age five! Both men and women employees during our study spoke of the great importance of their families in their lives. Many mentioned that despite the extended work hours necessary at start up and other critical moments in product development, they found flexibility of schedules and leaves supportive of family life.

When the work crisis at Tertia forced a major rescheduling of shifts and hours, this took a toll on employees' family lives—people had to start working on weekends as well as weekdays; child care dropoffs and pickups needed revision; afterschool schedules were in a mess. But most workers thought they could work out the kinks at home, and overall they felt proud that a product they had worked on for years was deemed a success and would be marketed. Their self-respect was enhanced.

When the layoffs occurred, the sacrifices made on the home front were felt by many to be no longer noble but naïve and maybe even stupid. Employees had indeed accommodated to change but in this case, for at least some of the workers, it backfired. Feeling self-respect under these circumstances is not easy.

GENDER LENS

The uneven development of self-respect also has a gender lens. In all of the biotech companies, there are still differences between male and female employees regarding the juggling of work and family responsibilities. The ideal worker is still thought to be someone who demonstrates commitment to the job by working on site and who has the flexibility to work overtime hours whenever necessary. Since women still shoulder the primary care-giving responsibilities on the home front, men are more likely to be able to achieve the ideal status. In biotech this has real meaning since over half of all the employees have either young children at home or care for elder relatives, or both. Having to choose between meeting family and work demands is not just a stressful exercise. It also diminishes a person's sense of achievement in either realm and sets up a lose-lose framework. If you see yourself not keeping up at work or at home, your self-respect is compromised.

The actual work systems in the biotech industry could permit greater flexibility with hours, scheduling, and telecommuting. And, indeed, the senior scientists have more autonomy to create more flexible time arrangements. But among professionals on the lower end of the ladder, there is less flexibility. This is especially true for the manufacturing workers and for the administrative support staff who are mainly women.

For all biotech employees, options for flexibility almost always are individually negotiated department by department or even supervisor by supervisor. A work-family program is not evenly distributed via an equal and fair systemwide approach. This lack of universal fairness is an issue that still plagues the biotech industry, though some of the sites have made greater strides than others in moving toward a more family supportive culture.

SOCIAL RESPONSIBILITY

It was a humid afternoon and I was talking to a male junior scientist about his work. He had considered a number of careers before winding up in biotech and provided this explanation for his strong work attachment: "Everything we do here is potentially terribly important and contributing to humanity. And even if we fail, we still learn something that's important."

His sentiments get to the core of what many employees say about their jobs in biotech—they have a value that is very concrete—you feel engaged in making a difference every day. If the product you are working on is a winner, you've made a difference. If it fails, you still have contributed to the knowledge learning curve.

The sense of doing work that has value to others links the ethics of social responsibility to individual dignity at work. And the notion of social responsibility is not just an abstraction for the biotech employee. They can picture a real person benefiting from their work. At Tertia, there is a video that employees can watch; it shows patients who have benefited from their product speaking about the lessening of their pain and regaining their independence.

At the other sites where the products are still in an earlier development stage, employees still experience a strong commitment to making a difference. As a woman biologist at Segunda stated, "The pharmaceutical companies aren't out to cure the roots. They are just out to make you feel better. Biotech is out to cure diseases. We're finding out how disease progresses and finding ways to prevent it from happening. I see that as a way to go and as having true value for society."

What is particularly interesting about her comment is her sense of pride that biotech is on the frontier of discovery. Unlike the pharmaceutical companies, she sees biotech firms as the true heroes, fighting for cures not just palliatives. This heroic position is reminiscent of the pride of air traffic controllers who saw themselves at work making sacrifices for the public good. For biotech employees, the trade-off is the balance between risk taking (both during scientific experiments and by working in a risky business that may not be here in five years) and the satisfaction of contributing something of true value to the world.

MAINTAINING BALANCE

Maintaining this balance is key to the dignity of a biotech worker's existence. One of the most significant findings from our study was how biotech workers compose a life that allows them to maintain this balance day to day, year to year. As we began our research, we assumed that biotech workers, as many other professional and information sector employees, would be quite mobile, moving from region to region when work options arose, and that they would see their community ties, if any, as part of national or even global networks. The bowling alone scenario described in chapter four was another force that we suspected would pull our relatively young workforce away from civic participation. We imagined our biotech workers as hard working professionals, as being deeply connected to social responsibility through the nature of their paid jobs but otherwise living typical suburban, disconnected lives.

We were wrong. Biotech workers have strong attachments not only to their families but also to a range of community networks. We came to understand that being rooted in community is a way that biotech employees deal with personal financial insecurity and industrywide vulnerability.

Interviews with biotech professionals show that many have rich, extended family networks and rely upon them for many aspects of care giving, including child and elder care. While the literature on professions has emphasized nuclear families, isolated in their privatizing daily life, our study revealed a combination of extended family networks and community organizational arrangements that created a web of support for our biotech employees.

The importance of extended family is a striking finding as many assume that this barely exists any longer in the new global economy. Many biotech professionals heavily rely on the social support from extended family members. For example, Maureen, a biotech manager, bought a house with an in-law apartment so her mother could help with the care of her daughter. Her mother used to care for her daughter one day a week—"Nana days"—cutting down on expenses of day care. Now that her daughter is in grade school, Nana brings her granddaughter to the bus each morning and meets the bus after school. Nana also takes care of her granddaughter during afterschool hours.

This extended family system raises the capacity of biotech families to deal with financial insecurities and the realities of dual-income or single-income households. It recreates a pattern of care giving that we saw in the early days of the industrial revolution, when extended family networks made the difference in keeping farm and factory families afloat. It also recreates the type of inner-city networks that kept lower income households in immigrant and people-of-color communities together. This fabric of networks, documented in Carol Stack's *All Our Kin* and Deborah Belle's *Lives In Stress,* seems now to be an integral part of the lives of middle-class professionals. Perhaps such social bonds have never disappeared but were made invisible because no one was expecting them to be there.

The pattern of reliance on extended family is partly due to the fact that many biotech professionals live near relatives—they either have lived in the region most of their lives, moved back to the region after a temporary stint took them away, or moved their parents to be closer to them after grandchildren were born. For many biotech professionals, the cluster effect of biotech work in the region has made proximity to relatives easier—major universities are linked to the biotech companies and thus form a seamless web of school to work.

COMMUNITY ATTACHMENTS

Attachment to community institutions is also a key feature of social connection for biotech professionals. Community of residence is the center for family activities. Child care, religious affiliations, and civic associations revolve around local communities not the work site. As for many Americans, affordable housing and quality schools are the key criteria for biotech families when choosing a community to live in.

The suburban landscape of community affiliations maintained by biotech workers reflects a trend in the country as a whole away from national organizations to more specialized, looser-knit, local-based activities. Local sports activities with children, local religious events, local civic associations provide the social networks. Few of the biotech workers are active in national political organizations or activities dealing with electoral politics. Biotech employees feel strongly about the roots they have made in their communities. Many chose to commute longer hours, sometimes up to two or more hours a day, rather than move closer to work. For instance, Fran commutes two hours a day, leaving her house at 6:30 A.M. and not getting home until 6:30 P.M. As a single mom, she appreciates the safety of her suburban community, its good school system, and the variety of activities available to her family—library story hours, town hall concerts, puppet shows. While she would like to shorten her long workday, the quality of life in her community reinforces her rootedness there.

When Segunda made its move closer to the Boston area, many employees expressed a reluctance to move. They cited more expensive housing prices closer to Boston as one negative factor. But their positive feelings about their communities were an even greater pull. Most had owned their homes for quite awhile and had formed meaningful ties to their children's child care centers and schools, to a network of doctors and dentists and other professional supports, to religious institutions, and to a web of friends and to family.

These are the ties that bind biotech people to social relationships that last over the years. The community connection exists alongside the ties of collegiality and friendship that most biotech workers report having at work. But the community ties are the connections that provide a deeper level of security since biotech workers are aware of the precariousness of their workplaces. Moving between the network of biotech firms is expected and increases the sense of wanting stability at home.

The pattern of ties to the community, we found, also reflects the gender nature of who in a family keeps up social relations. It is clear that women biotech workers are much more likely than their male colleagues to be involved in creating and sustaining relationships that integrate work, family, and community. Women undertake most of the informal community involvement, from attending parent-teacher meetings, to transporting children to activities, to volunteering in faith-based associations. The few men who are involved in a regular way in the community are more likely to hold formal roles such as serving on a school science committee or a town health council. They do not tend to be members of clubs such as the Lions and Elks.

For both male and female biotech employees, little community involvement takes place through formal institutions of community association that are part of larger political processes and national networks. As Theda Skocpol observed (see chapter four), there is an important difference between local, informal community links and the type of community associations that shape national policies and directions. While both are important in sustaining democracy, the biotech employees seem unconnected for the most part to the latter forms of association.

PUTTING IT TOGETHER

Biotech employees seem to have negotiated a way of achieving a livelihood, a sense of self-respect, and social responsibility within a workplace that is in constant change. For this reason, they mark for us a possible way forward in the emerging, rapid-paced global economy. The way is not perfect but it is hopeful.

As manufacturing workers, middle-level professionals, and senior scientists, they have secured wages and salaries that allow at minimum a decent standard of life and, in some cases, a sense of being well-off. Their access to a livelihood is better than some workers across America but representative of many others. As most Americans, the families of biotech workers depend upon two incomes to stay afloat. And while the way work is organized could provide options for work-family flexibility, these opportunities are not implemented systemwide. So a livelihood is achieved but moving beyond individual solutions to work-family tensions remains a challenge.

Biotech employees have achieved self-respect that grows from using their skills and knowledge on the job, from continually learning new ideas and methods, and from clear affirmation from their coworkers. They also report receiving respect for their work from their extended circle of family, friends, and colleagues. They are not unaware that their industry has been rebuked for protecting high drug prices that especially negatively affect the elderly and the critically ill. But despite the position of the companies on these matters, the workers see themselves as doing important work that deserves respect.

The biotech employees have a strong dual social responsibility connection: They have a strong, informal, home community-based connection to the type of small "s" social responsibilities that come from local associations; and they have ties to the larger "S" type of social responsibility—making a difference to society as a whole—which primarily comes from their workplace endeavors. Both are important to them as individuals. Both are important to sustaining our democratic society.

The balance of enjoying discovery and change on the one hand while creating a stable network of family and community ties on the other is perhaps the most intriguing lesson for us. It is one way for future workers to navigate the shifting world of work. On the one hand the biotech workers I interviewed enjoyed being on the cutting edge of discovery, and many saw themselves as explorers in the land of new drugs and new technologies. But, at the same time, biotech workers were quite traditional about other dimensions of their lives. They were tied to raising families and caring for children and elders.

Biotech workers, as many other American employees, say they are not very interested in uprooting families for reasons of work, even if it would mean a financial increase. In their search for dignity, they are thinking beyond the bottom line. They are committed to reaching for new knowledge and new experiments even as they keep themselves and their loved ones rooted in safe surroundings. The quality of life seems to be of utmost concern. The biotech employees, perhaps forecasting the workforce of the future, provide evidence of dignity that comes from "walking the talk" of values at work and home.

CHAPTER SIX

The Bank Story

If the employees in the biotech industry have learned how to maintain dignity while walking on Jell-O, the women and men in the banking industry have struggled to learn how to survive rather than sink.[1] With constant reengineering and restructuring resulting in massive layoffs, bank employees have had a tough time securing a steady livelihood. With major shifts in the nature of banking and how the work gets done, it has been difficult for employees to maintain pride in their skills and to reap respect from coworkers and supervisors. In a banking culture that primarily has been "mean and lean," time for family and for social responsibilities has been hard to find.

Today, the world of banking bears little resemblance to the old-fashioned image of staid old men in dark suits, austere and slow paced within echoing marble halls. In the intensely competitive world of international finance, banks face harsh threats from nonbank institutions such as brokerage firms and insurance companies. Both at home and abroad, commercial banks have lost ground to nonbank institutions. In fact, over 1,000 banks failed in the United States during the 1990s, more than any since the Great Depression.

It is no surprise, therefore, that the days when a career in banking was synonymous with stability have disappeared. For many decades, employees entered banking thinking they could have a job for life. Workers with a high school education often entered the bank at the ground level as tellers and were trained on the job to be generalists, familiar with all of the bank's functional areas. Gradually, bank employees worked their way up the career seniority ladder to achieve the level of branch manager and upward.

This well-known tradition of economic job security in banking is now a thing of the past. As I began my interviews with bank employees, one underwriter met me in the parking lot. As we walked toward the bank's entrance, he stopped me and looked up at the large letters atop the doorway. "See that name? Each day I look up and check just to be sure that overnight they haven't changed the name again." In his decade in banking, the name had changed four times. He said that he was a survivor, but barely. It is the human face in the global economy.

Banks today are caught in a whirlwind of uncertainty and heightened volatility generated by the deregulation of capital markets worldwide. The advent of floating exchange rates in the 1970s, the deregulation of U.S. bank interest rates in the early 1980s, and the new rules concerning cross-border banking—both interstate and transnational—have combined to dramatically increase international financial flows and intensify competition among both banks and nonbank financial institutions, now free to offer an expanding array of products and services.

To survive, the banking industry has been forced to consolidate operations to achieve productivity gains. The 1980s witnessed a tremendous wave of mergers, takeovers, and alliances among banks seeking economies of scale, industry dominance, and the right blend of new products and services.

For the customer, banking has been radically transformed. In the 1970s people would walk into their local bank and have the entire bank system offered to them by familiar faces of tellers and managers. These branches now function primarily as retail outlets, with traditional branch functions transferred to large data processing centers, 24-hour teleservicing centers, and "loan factories" for processing applications using assembly line techniques. When the customer calls one of these centers, if you reach a person and not a machine, you reach someone you will never see, someone who probably is located halfway across America.

For the employees, like the underwriter in the parking lot, the transformation of banking has meant facing job loss, losing colleagues, adapting to new corporate cultures often more frequently than changing cars. Overall in the past 10 years, commercial banks eliminated over 70,000 jobs. While the bulk of remaining jobs are still clerical, the share of these clerical positions has been shrinking. Traditionally, women have held the lion's share of these jobs, often due to their "mother's hours," but they have lost out as these jobs are reengineered out of existence due to widespread mergers and relentless automation of financial operations. From 1985 to 1995, 41,000 bank tellers lost their jobs.

The Bureau of Labor Statistics projects a decline of 10.4 percent in bank employment between 1994 and 2005. As additional branches close, mergers continue, and customers are pressured to use electronic banking, the overall number of jobs will continue to decline.

However, some workers will not only survive but will see their jobs expanded, redefined, and sometimes enhanced. As automation has displaced many of the lower skilled clerical jobs, mostly held by women, it has created new jobs, particularly for highly skilled systems analysts and technical personnel, mostly held by men. Banks' traditional personnel, like loan officers, now depend on credit scoring and other computer systems to perform their daily tasks, with more focus now on customized lending.

Thus, banks are increasingly looking for workers with more specialized skills, greater knowledge intensity, and abilities to adapt to constantly changing demands, widening geographic service areas, and multiple time frames. Indeed, instead of traditionally defined banking hours and the availability of "mother's hours" jobs, bank employees are often expected to operate closer to the 24/7 clock; available twenty-four hours a day, seven days a week.

Recruitment is often from the outside rather than from within the bank as was the case a generation ago. There is thus less internal upward mobility for lower skilled workers. The path that once led from the back office to the manager's chair has disappeared. Annual turnover rates in these occupations have exceeded 30 percent as the lack of job mobility and the increased pressure of forced overtime make these jobs less desirable. Even for those at the high end of the bank organization, there is little security in the new world where at any time the name above the door can change.

THE WORLD OF FLEET

In 1996 I gave a speech to Radcliffe alumnae and spouses in New York City on the "win-win agenda": How can we organize work so that we both attain business goals and meet family responsibilities? The how included discussions of reorganizing work so outcome measures are met beyond profit margins, such as respecting the time needed for family responsibilities and for civic involvement. Such reorganization of work would rely on knowledge input from employees on the best ways to accomplish their tasks, while managers, possibly after retraining, would be expected to offer cooperation and encouragement during the implementation of the restructuring of work. Moving beyond the bottom line would be a joint effort by individual employees who strive to attain dignity at work and by employers who understand the advantages of corporate responsibility for achieving family and democratic values. At the end of the dinner presentation, the CEO of Fleet Bank, Terrence Murray, approached me. "I am not sure I believe in your agenda, but I would like to talk with you further."

Two weeks later, I found myself at downtown Boston's Fleet headquarters. While awaiting lunch with Murray, the executive vice president for Human Resources, Anne Szostak, and I began a conversation about what a "win-win" or dual agenda could mean for Fleet. We quickly found ourselves discussing our own struggles with raising teenage daughters, caring for elderly parents, and holding down demanding jobs. By the time lunch began, it was clear a meeting of hearts and minds had occurred. CEO Murray, hearing about the costs of rising turnover and the increasing need to retain valuable women and men employees, agreed to an experiment to put a win-win agenda to the test at Fleet: Could employees and managers reorganize work to meet production goals and meet family and community responsibilities? Still skeptical, he said, "Show me!" The Radcliffe-Fleet Project was conceived by the end of dessert.

An interdisciplinary team of researchers was assembled at the Radcliffe Public Policy Institute. The first task for the research team was to select two sites in the company for launching the project. Research team members would learn from the employees about their work organization and life commitments and help them brainstorm a dual agenda: how to reorganize work so that it improves productivity *and* quality of life. Then, in each selected site, experiments would be set up to redesign how work got done. Finally, the research team would work with the employees at each site to identify evaluation measures to determine outcomes for the firm and for the individual employees. CEO Murray wanted clear, bottom-line measures to hold the dual agenda accountable. The team, not unlike a band of explorers, prepared itself to enter the world of Fleet.

FROM THE LOCAL TO THE GLOBAL

The biography of Terry Murray and the history of Fleet provide a parallel picture of rising fortunes. Born in blue-collar Woonsocket, Rhode Island, the son of a textile mill laborer, Terry's first job was working night shift in the mill during a year out from high school due to unruly behavior. Later, he entered Providence Country Day School on a scholarship and continued on to Harvard University. His Horatio Alger rise had started.

Upon graduation in 1962, armed with an English degree, he applied to 26 stock brokerages for a job but was rejected by all. Unfazed, he took a job at the Industrial National Bank of Providence. Terry slowly and methodically climbed to success, and turned the tiny bank in the smallest state in the nation into one of the nation's ten largest banks.

Fleet Bank's history during the decades of the 1980s and 1990s reflected amazing growth as the banking industry in general went through wholesale transformations. Formerly a single Rhode Island–based bank with $3 billion in assets, today Fleet is America's eighth largest bank with over $80 billion in assets. Its operations now extend from the Atlantic to the Pacific coast and across the continent to Latin America. Under the leadership of CEO Murray, Fleet has acquired or merged with over 75 banks.

At the turn of the century, Fleet had an expanding national presence in nontraditional banking activities, including insurance, brokering, and money management concerns. From its early days in the tiny state of Rhode Island, Fleet was forced to be entrepreneurial and reach out to other markets to survive. This push to diversify into other arenas gave Fleet an advantage whenever the opportunity arose to capitalize on market trends and the gradual easing of interstate banking restrictions.

The culture of rapid expansion and acquisition has been tightly linked to an environment of consolidation, cutting costs, and streamlining operations. Consolidation measures entail widespread branch closings, employee layoffs, and other cost-saving actions. Most notable in this respect was the "Fleet Focus," a massive cost-cutting, revenue-enhancing company campaign which eliminated almost 6,000 jobs between 1993 and 1996.

In 1997, Fleet announced that another 800 jobs would be cut in its branches, reducing the total number of Fleet employees to about 35,000. At the same time, Fleet intensified the pressure on its managers to slash expenses, forcing them to reexamine everything from computer systems to paper pads. To those inside and outside the company, Fleet had clearly reaffirmed its reputation as "a bank that runs by the numbers," an exciting but lean and mean place to work.

Fleet had also run into trouble with low-income and minority city residents regarding its mortgage lending policies. The bank was accused of red-lining, a practice whereby banks would not approve loans for properties in neighborhoods deemed undesirable and risky which were outlined in red markings on maps. These red-lined neighborhoods often were populated by racial and ethnic minority groups who felt discriminated against by the practice. Fleet thus had a legacy of being unfair to low-income, minority communities that added to its unfriendly reputation.

By the 1990s Fleet bank was already the largest bank in New England. With its $16 billion acquisition of BankBoston Corporation in 1999, Fleet officially became the eighth largest bank in America. As Fleet approached the new millennium holding $185 billion in assets, the bank estimated that 40 percent of future profits would come from its overseas business, investment management, and asset-based accounts. Fleet, increasingly big and diverse, faces the challenges of figuring out its future finance strategy and, perhaps more significantly, a basic approach to customers. Fleet has been known for its no-nonsense, bottom-line attitude while the acquired BankBoston had a consumer-friendly culture.

As the Radcliffe team prepared to launch the dual agenda experiment—an experiment to reorganize work so that both production goals and family and community responsibilities were met—this was the world of work we entered. The immediate reaction from most employees upon hearing about the experiment's goal of integrating quality of life and business objectives was one of disbelief. While most employees achieved a decent livelihood through their Fleet jobs, the tough culture of the organization made employees feel that the company cared little about their lives, families, and communities. The fact that CEO Murray had signed off on this project seemed counterintuitive, and the employees, echoing Murray, said, "Show Us!"

The team realized that if we could succeed in demonstrating that you could achieve a dual agenda in a Fleet-like culture, it would be a major victory, a real story of hope. We began by selecting two sites to house the project and surveying over 100 employees from the two sites concerning their work-life issues.

THE SITES AND SURVEY

On a beautiful New England day in October at a woodsy retreat center in Rhode Island, the research team leaders met with Anne Szostak and members of her Human Resources group. The meeting was in accordance with the research premise of collaborative participation. Unlike decisions done in a top-down fashion, the collaborative approach dictated that the research team, site managers, and site employees would work together to design the work reorganization experiment and also to determine project evaluation measures. This approach was built upon the assumption that the project's emphasis was less on programs and policies and more on the culture of the workplace: the practices and expectations that surrounded the accomplishment of the business goals in each site. The objective was to bring to the surface ideas that lay beneath the way work was organized in order to assess their impact on both the work and the lives of Fleet employees.

Another aspect of the approach was to focus on the system of organization of work—how work got done—and its effect on each worker in the unit. As such, the project looked at change that would affect the work group as a whole rather than a private accommodation between an individual and his or her manager.

Throughout the project we approached everything from the dual agenda, jointly looking at the needs of business and those of employees. We needed the cooperation from the managers and the rest of the employees. The combination of leadership buy-in from managers and close collaboration with workers was crucial for any success.

So as we began the process of selecting two sites for study, at the top of the priority list were the identification at each site of real work-life issues and the presence of identifiable business needs. In addition, we wanted sites that offered a wide distribution of employees in terms of sex, age, and race; a mix of exempt and nonexempt workers; the possibility of leadership support; and a geographical location within the greater Boston area where the research team lived. Because we had only less than a year to carry out, review, and write-up the experiment, we also decided to select sites that were not too large—50 or fewer people.

By the end of the retreat day, we had come up with four or five options and, after another month of investigation and discussion, decided on two sites, both valuable to the Fleet organization and representative of different aspects of the bank's functions: the Framingham site that was a Retail/Small Business Banking group and the Providence site that was a Reporting/Portfolio Management group.

Each site had experienced a significant amount of turmoil due to the constant changes at Fleet. The employees at Framingham had recently been relocated from their downtown Boston offices, had taken on more and more administrative tasks in addition to their underwriting duties due to cost cutting, and had not been able to establish reliable communication patterns with the sales representatives. On the work side, they faced increased pressure to work overtime, uneven workloads, and long commutes due to the relocation. These work realities spilled over into their homes with less time for family life and community participation and more personal stress. Working 12-hour days was common.

The employees in Providence faced a different set of difficulties due to Fleet's continuing acquisition and merger strategy. Their work focused on preparing accurate reports for internal customers within the bank. They were driven by the need to meet deadlines imposed by those outside their unit and to produce credible information. The integration of the accounting and computer systems of recently acquired banks posed difficult challenges given hardware and software technologies that often did not "talk" to one another. The unit also faced a greater demand for financial reporting on a more rapid basis, as the nature of their work changed from data processing to financial analysis. Members of the unit found themselves in a frenzied state, trying to meet deadlines by working long hours into the evenings and even on weekends. Family time and sometimes needed vacations were put off to meet a last minute demand for a report.

MORTGAGING OUR FAMILIES

To get a sharper snapshot of the work and life of the employees at both sites, the research team distributed a survey that 137 Fleet employees completed. We learned that the employees rated family as the central priority in their lives. Work and career was second to the emphasis on family. Reflecting national trends, the most common type of family was the two-earner household, and over half of the employees had children.

The striking paradox that the survey revealed was that although they placed family at the center of their lives, employees hardly had time for family—in terms of either quantity of hours or quality of hours. All employees surveyed worked full-time, often overtime, and 40 percent reported working over 50 hours per week. In addition, almost all partners of Fleet employees worked outside the home, with 71 percent also working full-time jobs! It is not surprising, therefore, that we learned from the survey that two out of three employees were not satisfied with their work-life balance. The more hours they worked the more dissatisfaction they reported.

On the home front, both men and women employees agreed that women were still doing the majority of work at home. Similar to most dual-income families in America, they had three jobs and two people to do them; in almost all the cases, women were doing more than time and a half. Men and women reported this contributed to work-family conflict that spilled into both life at work and life at home.

The Fleet employees reflect the battle for time that is rampant across America. According to the United Nations' International Labor Organization (ILO), American workers are putting in more hours than anyone else in the industrialized world. While the number of hours employees work has been decreasing in almost every other industrialized nation, American families have added six weeks' worth of time at work per year over the last 15 years. When workers feel stressed for time, it is not only in their imaginations that they feel they are running harder to stay in place.

The linkage to productivity is also instructive. More time at work has not necessarily resulted in greater productivity. The ILO report shows that although Japanese and Europeans work fewer hours than Americans, their productivity is higher. So, more is not always better either in terms of costs to the firm or in costs to the workers and their families.

For the Fleet employees and their families, time was not on their side. As one credit policy officer lamented, "Time! All of our jobs are like vacuums sucking up our lives."

Between long hours on the job and, for many, long commutes home, there was not much time or energy left for living. Indeed, the Fleet survey told us that the workload and long commutes were the two things most disliked about their jobs. As a male portfolio manager summed up, "We are mortgaging our families for our work."

OUT OF BALANCE

Nearly one out of three employees reported health problems that they attributed to stress from workload. Perhaps the most compelling stress-related issue was the lack of good sleep. Eighty percent of Fleet employees reported sleep disturbances due to work problems. Some employees reported being so charged up at the end of the workday that they could not get to sleep. Some awoke in the middle of the night after anxious dreams evoked feelings of running faster and faster or never getting things done. And there was a group who reported awakening at dawn and not being able to get back to sleep while going over lists of everything that awaited them at the office. They all knew that the sleeplessness ultimately affected not only their own health but also their level of productivity at work and the way they interacted with their children and partners.

The Fleet people mirrored the larger picture of sleep deprivation affecting millions of American workers. According to the Washington-based National Sleep Foundation, 40 percent of American adults say they are so sleepy during the day that it interferes with their activities. The National Commission on Sleep Disorders says five million workers fall asleep on the job every year and estimates that, in the United States alone, businesses lose more than $150 billion a year in productivity as a result of employee fatigue.[2] As American workers show greater signs of physical exhaustion, their work suffers and so do their lives.

The Fleet research team also spoke directly with the spouses and partners of the employees. They echoed concerns about stress, commuting problems, job uncertainty, and time pressures. One spouse suggested that "employers need to understand that people have families." The families of Fleet felt caught in the contradiction of a firm that wanted to profess itself family-friendly, but due to downsizing and constant work stress actually undermined family stability.

In terms of dignity at work, a mixed picture emerged from the Fleet surveys and family interviews. Fleet was seen as a good employer in terms of pay, benefits, and opportunity for advancement. However, even the access to a livelihood was tempered by the overhanging threat of layoffs at any time for everyone. If you were attached to Fleet, a livelihood was assured, but you could be set adrift with little notice. Trading time for money did not even offer the long-range job security that had been traditionally part of the banking industry. One woman commented, "We all saw people get laid off . . . Once you have lived through it, you are very skittish . . . Logically you think they will keep the best people but they don't . . . It is an interesting lesson: There is no security anymore."

Employees reported for the most part liking their jobs, especially the underwriters who saw themselves with skills that had been built up over the years. Providing good customer service was an element of work many took pride in, and it contributed to their sense of self-respect. And feeling support from good colleagues also played a role in building the kind of trust important for dignity, which emerges in daily small exchanges at the workplace.

But at the same time that some elements contributed to self-respect, such as utilizing professional skills and receiving acknowledgement from coworkers, the culture of Fleet undercut an overall sense of well-being. Dignity was threatened by feeling constantly off balance, not being able to experience a sense of equilibrium between work and life. The lack of balance left Fleet employees with a sense of vertigo—losing their lives as they worked harder and harder to succeed. They lacked a secure sense of livelihood; they lacked trust that their work skills would be respected; and they lacked the time for connection with their families. Disequilibrium undermined the attainment of dignity.

NO TIME FOR COMMUNITY

At Fleet, there was a distinct absence of employees talking about making a difference to the larger community. Unlike the biotech workers, the Fleet workforce did not see themselves as being on the cutting edge of innovation or contributing directly to the common good. For Fleet employees, that type of activity seemed to flow exclusively from community and volunteer commitments, such as working with burn victims at a Shriners' Hospital or participating in little leagues with kids outside of work time. And because of the long hours at work, most employees did not have the time and energy to follow through with such participation.

Having no time and energy for community activities has costs for the individual, for the firm, and for the larger society. For the individual, it removes the possibility of making a difference and reaping the benefits of social engagement. For the firm, the advantages of being viewed as a good "community citizen" are foreclosed. And, a society cannot sustain democratic values and practices unless citizens are active participants in civic endeavors.

Fleet employees were struggling to regain a sense of meaning in their lives for themselves and their loved ones. Like many white-collar workers, they were expected to work unpaid overtime. As cutbacks happened, they often had to pick up the slack, with managers expecting them to do more than one full-time job for the same one-job salary. Many worried that there was no way to limit the hours one put in without hurting one's career. And work extended to taking work home and being on call, even on weekends. Trading time for money was exacting a cost. Our Fleet respondents knew they were losing something valuable but felt stuck with no clear solutions in sight.

The research team launched experiments at two sites: Framingham and Providence. Because I was assigned to Framingham, I have chosen to focus on findings from that site.[3]

THE EXPERIMENT

In early 1996, 200 Business Banking Fleet employees were relocated from their Boston offices to an old Shawmut Bank building in Framingham, Massachusetts, about 30 miles west of the city. This was not a happy move. The manager of the unit had fought the move, knowing it would add commuting time for most employees, but cheaper office space prevailed.

The group as a whole focused on underwriting loans of all sizes. We chose the traditional underwriters group of 20 male and female employees as participants to design and implement the experiment. This group was in charge of underwriting the large loans of $100,000 up to $1 million.

The objective of the group was to build loan portfolios prudently with good loans. Productivity was usually measured by the quantity of loans processed per underwriter. But for underwriters, the quality of their performance was also measured by the quality of their loans and by customer satisfaction. The firm's focus on quantity did not take into account the emphasis on teamwork, mentoring, and peer reviews, which were used to ensure a high quality product.

The underwriters did not want their work to be valued only in terms of "making widgets." They had pride in their work, their skills, and their understanding of what it takes to make a good loan and keep their customers happy. The emerging Fleet focus on quantity made the underwriters uneasy, especially at a time in which they were taking on more and more nonunderwriting tasks and having their work segmented into fragments. The underwriters were worried that what it really meant to be a good underwriter was becoming lost in a climate that focused only on quantity not quality. They also feared for their future career growth.

The underwriter group identified to the research team three areas for creating change. The first had to do with improving how loans were administered. Bank cuts in support staff and the inability of Fleet's computer systems to keep pace with information processing needs meant underwriters were spending increased time doing clerical chores rather than underwriting. They spent hours writing commitment loan letters to customers, outlining the terms and conditions under which Fleet makes loans. This extra work meant longer workdays and a decreased ability to manage workloads.

New computer technology that could have made life easier was, in fact, making life harder. As Fleet mergers occurred during the 1990s, integrating the acquired computer systems into one coherent and efficient companywide operation was not going smoothly.

Sales reps out in the field and underwriters back in the home office could not easily exchange information and files via computer, resulting in more paperwork and frustration.

Next, underwriters felt uneasy about Fleet's decision to split the sales and underwriter functions. In earlier times, sales reps and underwriters worked out of the same office in regional teams. They were now split up and operating out of different locations. In addition, the sales representatives who dealt directly with loan customers did not always screen loans effectively and did not always send information to the underwriters in a timely and useful manner. If the underwriter did not have a good relationship with the sales representative, the work became much harder, extending the time it took to get a loan done, adding stress, and making it difficult to reach production goals.

Finally, because the recent move to the suburbs had added many more hours of commuting for a number of the underwriters, there was a strong interest in finding ways to decrease the strain of the added hours of travel on work time and family time.

THREE EXPERIMENTS

Three experiments were set up with the objective of achieving a mutual gain solution, improving the production of work and improving the work-life balance. Before and after measures were to be kept on each of the three new ways of working.

First, on the administrative overload, a small committee of underwriters developed a proposal that focused on how reorganizing work could reduce the hours spent on administrative tasks and free time for underwriting. This made a lot of sense, because underwriters were getting paid a professional salary to use their underwriting skills, not to do clerical work. Meanwhile, one administrative assistant was supporting all 20 people in the under-writing group.

The main focus of the experiment was to shift several adminis-trative tasks from the underwriters to the administrative assistant, who would in turn delegate some clerical tasks to a new employee, temporarily hired until the experiment could be evaluated. The temp would take on such tasks as delivering faxes and photocopying to free up the regular assistant to work on the commitment letters, which in turn would free up the underwriters to do underwriting!

Second, on the need for a better work arrangement between the underwriters and the sales representatives, two changes were tried. Before the changes, underwriters and sales staff were organized into regional subteams, with some pairs of underwriters and sales reps confronting difficulties caused by poor markets, poor training, or poor communication skills. Uneven workloads among the under-writers resulted in frustration and a sense of unfairness. One change thus involved underwriters being able to swap loans at their own initiative, even across regions. The management team also reorga-nized the group based on a review of individual workloads in order to spread assignments more evenly. Managers began to rotate oversight as their way of sharing the work load.

Telecommuting was the third idea that attracted many of the stressed commuter employees. Managers felt that the bank's sys-tems and information security systems limited options for extensive off-site working arrangements. There was also managerial hesitancy about the loss of "face-time"—people being in the office under supervision. But they were willing to try out a small experiment with two people—one working closer to home by working one day a week at a nearby branch office, the other allowed to work at home one day a week. To track their experience, both telecommuters completed weekly logs to get a sense of how changes in their work sites fit into the efforts of the group as a whole.

The cost to Fleet for all three of the experiments was minimal: the costs of a temporary worker for a three-month period and some furniture for the telecommuter set up in the branch office. During the three months, measures of productivity and work-life improvements were collected at the start and then in the middle of the experiments. The research team, managers, and employees anxiously waited for the final outcomes.

THE RESULTS

The first results were received from the administrative overload experiment. On a scale of 1 to 10, with 10 indicating a total success, the underwriters rated it an 8.8. What was most beneficial overall, according to the group, was the process of having a strong say in how work got done. There had been a change in the locus of power of who decided how work was accomplished, keeping in mind the dual agenda goals of business gains and gains for employees.

The underwriters had taken a joint look at what problems they faced in getting their work done and found some low-cost, relatively easy-to-make changes. And each piece of the reorganization of work had paid off. The underwriters were doing more underwriting; the administrative assistant felt her job had been upgraded as she took on the writing of commitment letters; and the temporary worker had proven her ability to take on the needed clerical tasks. The experience undermined the myth of either/or thinking that gains for employees are necessarily losses for employers. Mutual success had been achieved: By not having to stay at the end of the day to write commitment letters, underwriters could concentrate more on their loans, moving them along faster and at the same time doing better quality work. There were fewer complaints about inconsistencies and content errors.

On the home front, employees could go home earlier because the letter writing had not been piling up all day. One underwriter said he finally had time to spend with his new baby daughter, while another remarked that she now had time to make a home-cooked dinner for her family.

The loan reassignments experiment results came in next. At the first check, underwriters reported little improvement in their relationships with the sales reps and in the swapping of loans. But by the end of the three months, the group rated the changes as positive, a 7.6 on the 1-to-10 scale. Managers and underwriters both reported liking the rotation system of management oversight. Managers said it gave them a "more effective big picture," and underwriters thought they were able to manage their own backlogs better when they knew they could swap loans when it would be helpful. With better communication processes set up with the sales reps, there were fewer unplanned interruptions during the day. This translated into more concentration on doing the underwriting, more and better loan writing, and thus greater productivity. Managing the workload better also reduced stress for the individual underwriter, which many reported decreased the stress level at home.

For the third small experiment, telecommuting, the results were mixed. While both underwriters were positive about the change, the home telecommuter was more successful. She reported that the increase in uninterrupted time improved her productivity by allowing her to accomplish more in less time. In the beginning, she needed to learn how to organize her work so she could plan what to bring home. After she became adept at this, her only limitation was not being able to access certain databases at home due to security and other bank regulation issues.

On the quality of life side, our home telecommuter was very pleased. "I have more time to do the things I enjoy. I can eat at a decent time with my husband . . . I am not so stressed from the day and the commute, so I have regained my energy which helps me at home but also at work all week."

The branch telecommuter faced some unexpected difficulties since the branch was not well set up to accommodate her telecommuting situation. She had to change desks week to week and never had a fixed location to call her own. However, she reported feeling "like a different person" at home when she did not have to commute, and she gained time and energy to "do small chores at home and . . . to read." These small changes made a big difference in her overall quality of life, she reported. And her unit manager said that despite the obstacles at the branch, she was able to keep up with all of her work, and he was pleased with the productivity results.

This feedback loop—less stress at home generating more energy and thus more productivity at work, and less stress at work leading to more energy at home—was the single most important finding. Both Fleet and the employees were winners.

❖ ❖ ❖

When the research team began, we had not even thought of asking a question about sleep. However, the lack of good sleep due to stress at work kept coming up in early discussions. From the short surveys administered at the beginning and end of the experiments, we learned that disturbed sleep had dramatically decreased. In just the three-month period, the numbers of underwriters reporting sleeplessness decreased from four out of five to less than half. When this finding was reported at a later Fleet senior manager meeting, everyone in the room realized what a difference good sleep meant for day to day productivity. If any manager had doubts about accountability, the sleep measures alone were deemed remarkable.

But there were other measures of productivity gains as well. Turnaround time for loans met all the key production goals of the unit. Throughout the period, the average dollar amount per loan decision was maintained at the desired rate of close to a quarter-million dollars per loan. And, working the backlog down went more smoothly than ever before.

OWNING THE RESULTS

From the first fall day retreat a year before, the research team that entered Fleet Bank faced a wall of skepticism from the CEO, the managers and employees, and even from the family members. For a long time, people had bought into the either/or thinking that what was good for productivity necessarily was bad for employees' lives. Slowly, very slowly in the beginning, the managers and employees in the units chosen for the project learned a new way of thinking: Work could be reorganized so that business goals were met *and* family lives and community involvement could be enhanced.

But the learning was not easily assimilated as the larger existing bank culture was often resistant to change. It took a lot of risk taking by employees and their managers to shed old patterns of work and experiment with new ways of working that no one was sure would, in fact, work. A key element of change was the involvement of the workers themselves in the design and implementation of the reorganization process. The persistent patience, positive leadership, and courage to change were the significant factors that made mutual success possible.

Early in the research, I had commented to Anne Szostak, the head of Human Resources who had helped launch the project, that no matter the results, I wanted the courage of project participants to be recognized and rewarded by the most senior officials of the bank. As the experiment unfolded, participants became more and more excited about the changes they had given birth to at work. Word began to spread in an interim report in the company newsletter.

When the final results were in, I met with Terry Murray, the CEO, and, armed with quantifiable figures and data-driven reports, presented what we had learned. The time to celebrate the risk-taking work of the employees had come. So, early in the winter holiday season, just over a year after the project's launch, a party was held at the top of bank headquarters in Boston, with employees, managers, and their partners invited to feast on terrific food, with balloons and candy-filled mugs especially inscribed "Radcliffe-Fleet." For many employees, it was the first time they had ever been to the top floor of the bank. They heard speeches from their managers and their managers' supervisors praising their efforts. Terry Murray gave strong appreciative remarks. And Anne Szostak promised that the work begun in the two units would be carried forth into other areas of the bank.

❖   ❖   ❖

Those participating in the project felt they had done something of value for themselves, for others in the bank, and for their families. Both men and women had benefited from working in new ways. A degree of dignity, of feeling that through their own actions they could make a difference, was owned by participants. They had used their skills and knowledge to create a better workplace. They had gained respect for themselves. They had been given recognition by senior officials. Beforehand, they had been invisible, but now they were seen. Just as we saw in chapter one, dignity arises when patients in a hospital are seen and given the recognition that they deserve. The bank employees gained dignity at work.

Within the units of the bank that had experienced the risks and rewards of the experiment, questions remained about the durability of the gains. Would the changes endure and enlarge? For example, would more people be given the chance to telecommute, and would managers continue to work with employees to organize daily tasks to reduce stress? It was possible that after the intervention of the initial experiment wore off, the positive effects would be lost.[4]

Also, while the myth of either/or had been challenged at the unit level, the culture of the bank as a whole was the same as usual. The prevailing culture was still a culture that assumed profits, not people, count. If indeed there were productivity gains, would they be shared with employees or used to do more downsizing? The question remaining at the end of the project was how far would the bank go in embracing the new way of thinking.

. This was a well-implemented but small experiment. Like David and Goliath, the brave but small-scale changes were pitted against the imposing bottom-line bank culture. Would a new culture be adopted throughout the bank, causing major systemic changes in the way work was organized? Or would the experiments continue only in isolated units, occasionally replicated but not resulting in a major transformation in how work is done? As we begin this century, Fleet is just beginning to make a response.

The degree this bank story moves the search for dignity forward must be viewed by the meaning it has for our larger society. No doubt, firms that honor the risk taking and ingenuity fostered by the dual agenda approach will be better positioned to navigate the competitive, uncharted economic future that lies ahead. No doubt, employees who can enact the dual agenda strategy will be better positioned to achieve dignity at their workplaces. But as we will see in the final chapter, neither result is guaranteed.

SECTION

Future

THREE

CHAPTER SEVEN

Can You Work and Have a Life?

The question before us, "Can you work and have a life?" calls for an affirmative response from our minds and hearts, and even our souls. Over two hundred years ago, at another time that tried souls, Thomas Paine, in *Common Sense*, counseled the nation that "A long habit of not thinking a thing wrong gives it the superficial appearance of being right." There will be no victory in achieving dignity at work, no successful dual agenda of having work and a life without moving beyond the bottom-line thinking that holds us hostage.

Less than a mile from where I sit writing in Lexington, Massachusetts is the green where the shot was heard around the world. The march toward democracy had begun. Today, the social fabric necessary for sustaining democracy in our nation is being pulled apart, unraveled. Business as usual, which is organized to take people away from families and individuals away from social responsibilities, is a threat to our democratic values.

Democracy is sustained only when individuals feel society values them and that they are connected to the larger common good. Democracy survives only when the welfare of all the nation's families is secure, when men and women have sufficient livelihood and time to take care of those they love. Democracy flourishes only when the human right of dignity for each individual is understood as the basis for dignity as a nation.

Now it is time for our nation to march to the call of a different drummer, toward the right livelihood and the dignity we all long for at work, in families, and in communities. It is time to direct our energies to create work and working places that we and our children and our children's children deserve. Holding our organization of work accountable to human consequences is as important a measure of our country's effectiveness as market economic indicators.

Across the nation and rippling across the global economy, there are stories of hope that tell us that, by overcoming fears, by taking risks, and by keeping our eyes on the prize, transformation is possible and that it is coming. Change is occurring in the individual and institutional dimensions, through private initiatives and public policies. As individual practices and institutional efforts are integrated and private-public partnerships are implemented, steps beyond the bottom line toward dignity at work are being achieved.

For example, in Los Angeles County, 74,000 home health care workers who bathe, feed, and clean for the elderly and disabled, for the first time organized, with the help of their patients, to obtain benefits long denied them—health insurance and vacations.[1] They also obtained sufficient livelihood that allows them to support their own families. California public officials realized that, by raising wages and benefits, a more stable, better-trained workforce would create a win-win situation that would better the lives of the largely female minority and immigrant workers and allow the elderly and disabled to receive better care. Home health care workers and the disabled community together declared victory.

In the country's midland of Minnesota, St. Paul Companies, Inc., a provider of property insurance, has 90 percent of its workers on nontraditional schedules. Employees have choices of flextime, compressed workweeks, and job sharing.[2] The company provides twelve weeks of fully paid leave for new moms and two weeks for dads. Other noteworthy company-sponsored programs include summer camps for children, resources referrals, and backup child and elder care and pre-tax set asides.

On the East Coast, in the public sector Health and Human Services Agency in Washington D.C. and in a private law office in Boston, lawyers are experimenting with new forms of work including more flexibility to work at home or in offices closer to home by telecommuting, and the removal of billable hours as the measure of value to the organization.[3]

Beyond our shores, but touched by ripples of an American-led global economy, there are also hopeful signs. These signs are important for working Americans because our own work futures are increasingly linked to the fate of workers abroad. Divisions of labor by gender, for example, and inequalities of wealth between the haves and the have nots that exist abroad have mirror images in the United States. With new technologies and new communication systems, conditions of work in one part of the world have consequences for workers on the other side of the planet. If the shirt on your back is made by a worker in sweatshop conditions in Central America, if the computer specialists your company needs are easier to find in New Delhi, then work conditions and work opportunities here in the USA are affected.

In India, SEWA, the Self-Employed Women's Association, represents those who are among the poorest workers in the world.[4] They fall outside the conventional notion of employees and therefore outside rights, protections, and social security systems that exist in the world today. These women do not have one employment at one time. Instead, in any given week, 40 percent do two types of work a day, 25 percent do three types and 14 percent do four or more types. For example, one SEWA member spends part of her day doing piece-rate home-based work, is employed part-time as a salt worker, and also raises farm produce. It is the combination of all these tasks that gives her a marginal livelihood. SEWA is giving workers hope that new international policies will adopt new definitions that cover all workers and move everyone towards a base of economic security.

For many in America, this story of hope from India hits home at a time when the rewards of a booming economy have been so unevenly distributed, when many of us are indeed working so many hours, often in more than one job, and when so many of us work in fluid situations with no standard contracts of loyalty or commitment. In a global economy, workers here and abroad face the private and social costs of contingency work arrangements and the great inequities of the distribution of wealth.

The following longer story of hope is shared to help us focus our eyes on the prize and inspire us to create new ways of working.

THE NORSK STORY

In the faraway land of Norsk, people had a lot going for them. They had the highest standard of living of anyone on the earth—beautiful homes with all the latest technology, healthy children and long life spans, and lots of natural resources to keep things going well for seven generations ahead at least. Small farms dotted the landscape, the selling of land for development was discouraged since family ownership was seen as vital for their future. White-collar workers and professionals often still lived on farms where they had grown up and commuted to work in the city.

But there was trouble in paradise. No one had time to be in the nice homes and farms. Parents did not have time to play with their healthy children. Family, cows, and fields were being neglected. Everyone was rushing around, running faster and faster to stay in place, always trying to find time. Travel from the beautiful homes to the workplaces in the city was one big traffic jam each day, making everyone grumpy. And pollution was filling the air people needed to breathe and was contaminating the waters needed for drinking and for the wonderful fish people ate. Something needed to be done.

Together the people from Norsk came up with a vision. It did not just happen but came out of months and months of hard work, operating in committees, in small groups and large groups, battling through points of difference and through confusion. They wanted a practical view for the future—people would still work, have families, and think about their country's comparative advantages. But the prime notion, the new way of thinking underlying the vision was "balance is healthy." The folks from Norsk decided to redesign work to promote balance; not balance like a tenuous position in the middle of a see-saw, but balance as a sense of being centered, focused on what truly matters. They wanted to work in ways that would enrich family and community life.

Coming up with a practical vision was not an act of magic. It came from a combination of courageous leaders who moved out of the box of familiar constraints, committed organizing of the people of Norsk to participate in voicing their concerns and hopes, and a common conviction that together, a united people could create new ways of thinking that would lead, step by step, to innovative institutions. They knew important changes would not happen in one day but through incremental, tough work with lots of learning from trials and errors, like any good experiment. But they understood that since they had the will, they would find a way forward.

So, armed with a common practical vision, they shifted gears. Instead of short-term quarterly reports, they thought long-term. Office spaces were designed to help people gain sacred time to get work done in private that needed to be done that way and also to promote interaction when teamwork was needed. Good communication and teamwork were highly regarded and were understood as necessary to foster innovation and creativity.

People had flexible schedules so that they could take care of things at home and work. And the newest technology was employed, not to add new burdens to everyone's stress, but to make jobs more appealing and to keep a better balance between work and life. If someone from Norsk was still sitting at their desk at 6 P.M., folks wondered why they could not get the work done in the regular seven-hour workday. Working longer hours was no longer heroic. Balance was the key to being successful.

What is remarkable about this tale is that this story of hope exists in reality, in our time. Norsk Hydro is a company of 39,000 people, operating in 70 countries around the globe.[5] It is the world's second largest producer of oil from the Norwegian North Sea and the single largest salmon farmer. Their products are used in Cadillac bumpers, in Nokia cell phones, and as fertilizer on Florida tomatoes.

While going global with its products, the company is trying to make work life function for people at home. Like the biotech employees, the management and union people at Hydro are on the cutting edge of the emerging economy, attempting to create a new balance between product discovery at work and healthy family and community lives. Like the bank employees, they are risking new ways of working to implement a new balance. But unlike both sets of workers in the United States, the Norsk Hydro employees have comparative advantages: a systemic, companywide investment in their experiment by employers and employees, and, importantly, a culture that holds balance as a societal value. Balance is understood to be a social and an economic imperative.

❖   ❖   ❖

So far in the United States, we have continued to plunge ahead doing business as usual. The costs of this are ignored, rendered invisible by economists who prefer to stick with equations that disregard the "externalities"—the costs of unemployment, under-employment, and overwork, the costs of people at work without an adequate livelihood, self-respect, or the chance to fulfill social responsibilities.

But the costs of the loss of dignity at work are real, if complex. The individual and social costs are not easy to measure, but they show up in children and elderly parents left without care, in community activities with no volunteers, and in elections with few voters. For example, when working parents do not have time to spend with their children, children's educational achievement suffers; when employees do not have the freedom to spend time with ailing parents, the elders' health suffers. These outcomes have individual and social costs. If no one has time to volunteer to be a big brother or big sister, thousands of young people are left without role models and left with a feeling of disconnection from the larger world. This anomie and despair, as social scientists have documented, can lead to a rise in suicide rates and violence. These outcomes have individual and social costs. When an election is held and most citizens do not have the time or interest to be involved and do not show up at the polling booths, the costs to democracy are real. The human face of a bottom-line global economy has many costly images.

We have come full circle in our search for dignity at work. Back in the Garden of Eden, Adam and Eve struggled in their toils, as tillers of the earth and as parents of two children. As their descendents, we are engaged in a similar struggle for dignity, albeit at a different point of human history, in an economic world that has expanded from a garden to the globe. We are still human beings for whom dignity at work is an essential right.

A world without work is not only a fantasy; in our culture, it is a dangerous fantasy. My father's story in the preface of this book, substantiated further by evidence from other unemployed men and women, put forth the terrible private and social costs of job loss. And our discussion of the three pillars of dignity brought home how central work is for individual self-respect, for the well-being of families, and for the sustenance of democratic life. We know from social history that when work breaks down and does not serve the basic needs of the people, the ground becomes fertile for discontent, intolerance, and even fear.

The question that demands our attention is whether we can work in a way that enhances our chances for having a life with dignity—a life resting on the three pillars of gaining a decent livelihood, interacting with others to encourage self-respect, and making a difference through social responsibility.

There are significant signs of hope stirring in America. If we pay attention to these signs and act with courage and conviction, we will be able to respond to the next generation and the generation after that, "Yes! You can work and have a life." This is a wake-up call for us to respond with affirmation.

VOICES OF YOUNG AMERICANS: SIGNS OF HOPE

The younger generation is presenting signs of hope. Young people understand that work has always defined, to some degree, human existence, but that so much depends on how we handle our relationship to work—what values shape the why and the how of our work lives. For the first time ever in human history the majority of young men and women have been raised in households where both parents or single heads-of-household parents have held paid, outside-the-home, full-time jobs. They have experienced the realities of their parent's generation, frantically struggling to hold down jobs, raise kids, and take care of elders while being stressed physically and mentally. They see this as unhealthy and they do not want to replicate the pattern.

Signs of Hope: Gender Role Change

A surprising and stunning finding of a recent national survey, "Life's Work: Generational Attitudes toward Work and Life Integration," found that for young men in their twenties and thirties, having a work schedule that allows for time to spend with their families is their top job priority.[6] This is a gender role shift of major proportions. It promises to have significant effects on how work and family life are organized.

Young men are joining young women in wanting to have good jobs *and* time for raising children and going to community events. These young men do not wish to spend their lives working like their fathers and grandfathers, repeating the formula of being a never-at-home dad. They want to be there for their children and they want to be equal partners with women in care giving.

This potential realignment of male work-family roles could bring about a fundamental shifting of how we think of care giving in our culture. Providing care would be seen as socially useful and as productive for society as commercial work.[7] If men are serious about assuming an equitable share of child and elder care, then all forms of labor will require redistribution and reorganization. No longer seen as only a women's issue, reducing or making more flexible work schedules for all would address this in the workplace. Overtime hours would be voluntary, and when taken workers could chose between compensatory time or extra pay. To help in the transformation of gender roles and to validate care giving as socially productive, care-giving skills could be built into all educational levels for girls and boys, from the elementary to the university years. All of our young people would become adept in care-giving skills along with other skills necessary to be productive members of society.

Signs of Hope: Self Respect

In the "Life's Work" survey of over 1000 workers, both young men and young women placed strong value on the importance of having workplaces that offer opportunity for self-respect and social responsibility. On two indicators essential for self-respect—"doing work that allows me to use my abilities" and "having a good relationship with coworkers"—98 percent of young people responded that each measure was important to them. Also, 92 percent of the young people affirmed that "doing work which helps my community and society" was also important as a work value.

These young people understand that being able to use your skills at your job and getting respect from coworkers makes work dignified. Many of them during their school years knew the pain of being "dissed" by their peers and of having the stress of never being good enough to meet all the expectations of a highly competitive society. They want jobs that allow them to use their skills and to be creative. They want jobs in which they can work with others in productive ways and where they are treated with respect by their coworkers. The difference from previous generations is that they want this despite facing an economy that embraces insecurity and a culture that pushes "competitive individualism" as never before.

Many of these young people are now in nonstandard jobs— part-time, temporary, leased, or contract work. Half of all temporary workers in America today are 20 to 24 years old. While some young workers prefer nonstandard job flexibility many more would prefer to have full-time jobs that offer better wages and benefits. For noncollege graduates, who make up three-fourths of workers age 18 to 35, the opportunity to enrich and fully use skills and abilities is limited by placement in situations where they are expendable and easily replaced. Young people do not deserve a future where they will be invisible at work the way Simone Weil was in her factory job, Judith Rollins in her domestic servant job, and Primo in his office job. To be invisible is to be left without a sense of self-efficacy, without agency, without the ability to act on one's own behalf.

To ensure that young people can fulfill their hopes to have work that promotes self-respect, we need to create an educational system that makes college affordable to everyone who wishes to attend, that honors those who enter the trades, craft, and arts fields, and a work system that offers all people decent wages and benefits. For example, Martin Luther King, Jr., reminded us that the work of garbage workers, from those in the street to those handling hazardous waste, should be valued. These workers may be considered as part of our medical system as they clean up our environment. And we also will need to create intermediary institutions that span the life course and assure a generation of hopscotching, self employed, and nonstandard workers that they have the security necessary for sustaining self respect.

Signs of Hope: Social Responsibility

Young people in their late twenties and early thirties—those of generation X—have been labeled by the media as the "me" generation—self-absorbed and materialistically driven. But a different picture emerges from the "Life's Work" survey in which generation X members strongly voiced their desire for work that helped their community and society as a whole. These survey results echo the voices of young adults in focus groups I conducted in 1999, who described their ideal jobs. "I want to save the world somehow, perhaps like Rachel Carson, as a marine biologist," said one. "I've always been completely horrified by how much injustice in the world there is . . . so I have hoped I could be the one to fix that . . . maybe as a judge on a local level," responded another. "I can remember wanting to be a pediatrician for as long as I can. That pleased my mother who named me Alexandra—which means the helper of mankind. So I always wanted to be a helper of children," said a third.

There are a number of interesting patterns among these generation X focus group participants. They had seen images of the global economy through the news and media, images that disturbed them and made them think about the dichotomy between their own mostly middle-class lifestyles and the lives of those in impoverished circumstances and those who were subjected to conditions of war and injustice. When I was growing up, I heard about the poor children in Korea and later in Selma, Alabama. For generation X and the later generation Y, there have been stark televised images of starving children in Ethiopia, inner city poverty and violence in movies like *Boyz 'N the Hood,* and internet conversations with their peers in Kosovo as bombs were falling in the former Yugoslavia.

Like the generations before them, these young adults also had role models, particular people whom they saw doing the kind of meaningful work they wished to do—the Rachel Carsons and Nelson Mandelas of the world. Since they had seen the fruits of these people's labors, they could imagine themselves traveling a similar path: "If you see it, you can dream it."

The great value of having deep community ties was recognized by these young people. They shared the outlook of the biotech workers, who, despite being on the cutting edge of twenty-first century innovation, maintained very traditional roots in family networks and community-based activities. The virtual reality chat rooms and internet networks frequented by young people did not dislodge their desire for face-to-face human interaction and a sense of home and place.

One young woman spoke of her mother who is a minister and a single parent. Her mother taught her the importance of community connection:

> Our church is doing very well and the congregation said to my mom, "Why don't you move to a larger house?" But my mom refused, saying that this was her neighborhood. I see in my own childhood how much I was raised by a community

of people—everybody knows my brother, childcare arrangements are always taken care of, and when he gets locked out, someone has the key. If my mom moves she loses all that.

The demise of community ties is a serious concern for both individual and societal well-being. This young woman was, in fact, worried that she might not be able to compose a life of community roots like her mother's:

> I just don't see that happening for myself. Everything I need I have to buy. I have to find people who won't rip me off. It's incredible to search out a community so that you don't feel so overwhelmed by the things that used to be done by family and friends. And I don't think you can buy community . . . it is something you have to invest in.

She understood well that her own health and safety were in jeopardy in a world that usurped community. In the global economy, most businesses no longer have local community links, with market chains replacing smaller, family-owned establishments. New technologies mean that you are more likely to get automated replies to personal queries than a real human response. When you walk into a store or a bank, no one remembers you, and the good customer service you once enjoyed is undone by encounters with a series of constantly replaced workers.

In addition to the costs on the individual level of no one knowing your name in daily life activities are the larger social costs of community devolution. In an intriguing article in the *New York Review of Books,* Helen Epstein traces the relationship between population health and cohesion in social life.[8] She recounts a story from economist Richard Wilkerson's book, *Unhealthy Societies,* about a small town in Pennsylvania settled by southern Italian immigrants in the 1880s. During the 1950s doctors discovered that the town's residents died of heart attacks at half the natural rate, despite the fact that residents smoked heavily and consumed vast amounts of lard and other fatty foods, and that Italians from other Pennsylvania towns had heart attacks at the rate of other Americans. The secret for health, according to sociologist Stewart Wolf, was the quality of community life in the town. "You go down the street and everyone says 'Hello! Hello!' Every one was known by their name." By the 1980s, the town had changed, young people had moved away, families had dispersed, and the heart attack rate had risen to meet the national average.

Epstein's review suggests that societies in which there is strong social cohesion and a reality of egalitarianism are healthier than ones where these are missing. Our young woman was fortunate to have a community of adult supporters, and her brother could always find someone at home in the neighborhood. But in an economic world where single parents have to work long hours, often at two jobs, to gain a decent livelihood and dual-income household members are each working 50 or more hours per week to afford decent housing, health care, and education for their children, there is frequently no one home. People in neighborhoods often no longer know each other, so that while children are detached from their parents, the parents are detached from the larger community.

The costs to our society of thousands of latchkey children— kids who come home each day after school or part-time jobs to find no one at home—we are only beginning to comprehend. But we do know that children's reading skills are impaired when parents don't have time to read them books, that children's sense of belonging is diminished when families never eat meals together, and that children's sense of anomie—feeling isolated and alienated—can lead to deviant and dangerous behaviors that cost society dearly.

For lower-income families, the burden of keeping the family together in the absence of parents and community ties often falls to the daughters of the household. The continuing high rates of unemployment and prevalence of low-skill, low-paying jobs in racial minority and immigrant communities unravels the social fabric necessary to maintain strong families and a belief in the fairness of our democracy. As Lisa Dodson's thoughtful research documents, the care-giving responsibilities for younger siblings and disabled or incompetent elders fall all to often onto the shoulders of teenage girls, who have to give up any claim to their own lives to keep their families going.[9] The media and society have not infrequently labeled these girls—who sometimes drop out of school and look for love wherever they can find it—as "losers" and "immoral." Instead they may be acting heroically in the face of an economy and a society that does not provide them any respect, security, or reason to hope. They are providing the invisible work support system that makes the visible work front possible. We are thus undermining the very thing we are leaning on.

We need to drop the erroneous stereotyping of younger workers. Generation X young adults from middle-income homes are voicing their readiness to take on risks: young men wanting to make major gender role shifts to ensure they will be family care givers; young women striving for fairness, for equal pay, and for recognition in the workplace; both men and women committed to making a difference in the world around them by valuing others they work with and valuing the communities they live in.

And young people from lower-income backgrounds are already taking on burdens beyond their years and asking for a fair shake in facing the future. They too have shown strong commitments to family values and community ties, from helping to raise their younger siblings when parents have been absent, to doing hours of volunteer community service work in local neighborhoods. Through religious organizations, health clinics, and local youth groups, they are trying to knit together their own safety nets as outside sources of support have disappeared. We need to applaud the pragmatic idealism and readiness of generation X and Y-ers to change the world.

What we used to term "the sixty-four thousand dollar" question is whether we can create new institutions of work that will respond to these signs of hope and enhance the prospects for working and having a life: work that honors family life, work that honors gender role change, work that honors community-building, and work that honors principles of fairness and equality that are the mainstays of a democratic society. In other words, can we move beyond individual struggles to have dignity at work—struggles like Kate's decision to go from full-time to part-time lawyer; Dan's struggle to change industries so he could use his skills; Joan's struggle to go back to school to earn better wages? These are noble individual strivings and they are important in the search for dignity. But they are not sufficient. If our society is to stand for human dignity, then we need to have our institutions, including our work institutions, be places of dignity. And here again, there are signs of hope.

INSTITUTIONAL SIGNS OF HOPE

There are many signs of hope in America today that can be seen as building blocks for a new culture of work; in some instances they correspond to a new set of institutions and policies. A majority of these important changes are occurring on local and regional levels, not yet reaching national visibility. But they are significant because, as signs of hope, they can further stimulate our risk taking and because they make what some would call fantasy or idealism a reality that can be encouraged, enacted, and enlarged.

Among the more relevant signs of hopeful answers to our question of "Can you work and have a life?" are efforts on four fronts: overtime; portable benefits; care giving, and economic security. These efforts speak in powerful ways to the issues of livelihood, self-respect, and social responsibility that are the pillars of dignity at work.

Signs of Hope: Organizing to Overcome Overtime

On June 8, 1999 an airline copilot filed a grievance seeking better enforcement of crew rest rules.[10] He reported an incident that occurred during an overnight flight to Central America in the Mexican skies: "When I woke up, I looked over at the captain. He was sound asleep." Miraculously, no difficulties took place, unlike a week earlier when an airplane crashed in Little Rock, Arkansas, killing ten passengers and the plane's captain. He and the copilot on that flight had been on duty 13.5 hours, a half-hour short of American Airlines maximum duty time.

The Allied Pilots Association filed its grievance with the Federal Aviation Administration to ensure the safety of pilots, passengers, and airplanes. The FAA took the complaint seriously and said, in the future, strict adherence to overtime regulations would be enforced. The case represents an alarming but clear trend of how both the business goals of productivity and the quality of life issues of health and safety, for the individual and for the public at large, are endangered when people are forced to work overtime hours beyond their capacity to function effectively.

In the current global economy, a well-known ethic of the bottom-line mentality is that time is money. This mentality is coupled with rapidly changing technology that speeds up time—time for products to get to market, time to respond to orders and e-mails, time for financial markets moving toward round-the-clock and electronic trading. And in a period of skilled labor shortage, employers prefer to compel overtime from workers rather than pay wages and benefits and train new workers. In the United States, workers labor nearly 600 more hours per year than their counterparts in Norway, the scene of our story of balance at work, and almost 400 more hours than those from supposedly work-obsessed Germany.[11] So the push for overcoming overtime is happening not only in the air, but across the service sector, the manufacturing sector, and the information sector.

Successful battles are now being waged and won to counter this push for mandatory overtime. What all workers want, male and female, is for the choice of overtime—whether to earn extra money or have more time off—to be theirs. In the last few years, workers in the manufacturing industries of auto, steel, mining, and beverages have gone on strike, largely about mandatory overtime issues, and have won concessions at the bargaining table. During negotiations, it was pointed out that working long overtime hours causes greater rates of on-the-job stress, sickness, and accidents—all of which raise business productivity costs while also exacting tolls on an employee's quality of life.

In the service sector of the economy, we saw how the underwriters at Fleet Bank were able to reduce their long hours by restructuring work. Production goals were still reached and workers reported gains for their nonwork lives. Across the New England region, in another service industry, nurses were successful in overcoming mandatory 16-hour shifts.[12] At St. Vincent's hospital in Worcester, Massachusetts, the nurses facing these long shifts had great difficulty meeting both their family responsibilities and their job demands. The hospital had wanted to change nurses shifts and hours without notice. But day care providers do not work double shifts, and all care-giving services need to be planned in advance. After years of professional training, the nurses did not want to be treated like teenagers working a summer job. They also were concerned about their patients being treated by overstressed nurses who would not have the time or energy to do proper care giving.

The nurses' resistance to forced overtime was joined by the media and public at large. The larger community saw what was at stake and that fairness to the nurses would mean better health for the entire local population. A newspaper editorial opined, "At a time when American hospitals are struggling to reduce the toll of up to 100,000 accidental deaths that occur in their wards each year, it is a step backward for a hospital to require its nurses to work 16-hour shifts."[13] The Worcester community also spoke up, "People are uncomfortable, to put it mildly, with the bottom-line mentality that has come to dominate even the nonprofit sectors of the health care industry . . . We believe that health care providers are being asked to do too much with too little help, and we believe that patient care has suffered as a result."[14] This story illustrates a major step forward toward the goal of balance which unites care givers and the larger community.

The trend to work long hours has been pronounced in the field of information technology.[15] There is a sense that a 60-hour work week is a de facto standard. During the summer of 2000, Verizon Communications, the company created by the merger of Bell Atlantic and GTE, serving 25 million East Coast customers, reached an agreement with its employees on a number of work conditions including overtime. Forced overtime had been a major concern of the employees who often had to show up for work for more than 20 extra hours per week to keep their jobs. Under the agreement, similar to those reached by the Communications Workers of America in other regional negotiations, overtime would be limited to 16 hours in a week during the first year of the new contract and down to 8 a year later. Limits were also put on the number of weeks in a month that employees could be expected to work overtime. In an agreement with U.S. West, the CWA negotiated a contract that guaranteed two weeks per month without any overtime. This is still a lot of overtime but, as our people from Norsk learned, sustainable change happens through a series of steps forward toward a greater goal.

❖   ❖   ❖

Kate, our lawyer in search of dignity at work, gave up a full-time job for part-time status so she could work and have a life. She felt a sense of agency and efficacy in her individual movement. She was also fortunate that she could afford to work part-time. But the accounts above provide hope that we can achieve a wider shift in overcoming the tyranny of forced overtime. We can aim for systemic, institutional solutions. Indeed, Kate was not alone in her sentiments about not wanting to live to work. The Boston Bar Association itself recently called for a "cultural revolution" and now urges firms to move away from the number of billable hours as a measure of success. Instead, it counsels law practices to make sure their employees and partners have time for families, and to make sure they will still be able to have meaningful work and the respect of their colleagues. Kate made a small step forward for her dignity and now it is up to the firms to take the larger step. For the realization of dignity at work, individual acts of courage and change need to be connected to institutional initiatives and innovations.

Signs of Hope: Promotion of Portable Benefits

Changes in the economy and the way work is organized require that we think about health care coverage and pension in new ways. Both kinds of benefit are important aspects of livelihood and without them people cannot experience a sense of well-being and security in their lives.

As we explored in chapter two, the traditional employment contract, by which loyal employees provided labor in exchange for fair wages, benefits, and job security from their employers has almost disappeared. In its place the global economy has produced major corporate restructuring and new forms of work that embrace technological advances and nonstandard positions. According to the Department of Labor, over a third of American workers today do not hold traditional full-time jobs, but instead work as temps, consultants, or part-timers.

Women, who are the most likely workers to hold part-time and temporary positions, are particularly vulnerable. Fewer than 25 percent of retired women have pension coverage, compared to over

50 percent of all retired men. Women's social security benefits tend to be lower than men's as well, due to lower average pay, shorter job tenure, more family responsibilities, and working in smaller companies. And 25 million working women today have no retirement benefits at all.

Moreover, as we saw from the story of the biotech workers, even workers who hold full-time employment are often hopscotching from firm to firm, carrying their portable skills on their backs from company to company. And, electronically connected freelancers, some of whom rarely leave their home offices, do not even have to hopscotch to connect to another place.

All of these workers in the global economy still search for ways to gain security and meet their livelihood needs, which include benefits for their families. Dan, our accountant in the biotech industry, enjoyed many of the key ingredients of dignity at work— decent wages, the chance to utilize his abilities, and the time for family life. But he was still concerned about overall security in the hopscotch world he worked in, especially in regard to pension and health care for his family.

This diverse group of workers is not well served by either employer-based or independent benefit plans. A sign of hope is the birth of a set of emerging intermediary institutions and agencies that are creating portable funds that workers can count on as they move during their work lives from job to job.

Working Today is a recently founded organization that has taken a lead in providing low cost health insurance for freelance technology workers and portable retirement plans for workers in the new media industry in Manhattan. Its Portable Benefits Fund provides independent workers access to group rates and the ability to carry benefits across jobs. The fund delivers affordable health insurance and pre-tax retirement plans, including an annuity product whose initial contribution is only $25. This means that workers at all income levels can begin saving. The Working Today initiative drew upon the earlier model of the Screen Actors Guild which had long provided portable insurance for its members.

Given the changing demographics of America's labor force and the changing nature of work in the global economy, the concept of portable benefits seems a matter of common sense. But current public policies remain stuck in a time warp, still assuming that workers get insurance from employers who finance coverage. Employers are still able to deduct insurance costs from their expenses while workers such as temps and part-timers can deduct none. Present policy also does not permit independent and hop-scotching workers from combining employer, state, and personal funds to cover insurance premiums.

Many people are watching the portable benefit experiments launched by Working Today and applaud their vision and risk taking in tackling this significant dimension for achieving economic security. The success of the venture will be at least partly shaped by how wise public leaders will be in revising policies so they too can catch up to the new realities in working America. The success of our individual and common search for dignity at work rests on a creative blending of personal initiatives, organizational innovation, and intelligent public policy.

Signs of Hope: Valuing Care Giving

There will be no victory in achieving dignity at work, no effective dual agenda or win-win strategy without our recognition that care giving is as socially productive and important as commercial, profit-oriented work. The issue of care giving was a part of the story of Adam and Eve, who balanced their work with raising Cain and Abel. The important thread of care giving was woven into the reports of female and male workers throughout history, on farms and in early factories, in law offices and biotech labs, striving to have good work and family lives. Each age produced its own resolution to how people got their work done and took care of their families and communities. Individual stories varied, depending on not only what time in history you were born but also your economic status, your gender, and your race or religion.

Today, we continue this effort of getting up each day to work and also getting up each day to care for those we love and to keep our communities going. But there are unique challenges in the current economic order that call for reconsideration of how our daily lives are organized. For the first time in American history the majority of children are being raised in households where either both parents are working full-time outside the home or where a single parent—almost always a mom—is in charge. Parents feel their time is fractured by the pulls of private and public lives, and in each sphere they are spread too thin. Children and elders who need time and care are left too often today without either.

Traditionally, women have provided the sustaining care for families and the volunteer service that maintains community life. This care-giving labor was both difficult and satisfying. But being women's work, it was always devalued. Productive work came to be associated with the wage-earning work assigned to the public world of men. And even when women entered the public domain of work, they usually found jobs in the service, care-giving sectors. The majority of women in the United States are clustered in the service occupations of teacher, health care worker, sales clerk, and administrative assistant. In the bottom-line mentality of the global economy, the devaluing of care-giving work has intensified. We have seen the struggles of care-giving workers to maintain their commitment to patients and customers and to their own ethics and dignity. For example, even doctors are forming unions in the face of the bottom-line pressures from managed care firms to prioritize profits rather than patient care.

In the past, health care workers, like those who successfully organized in Los Angeles for better work conditions, received no training, and given their low wages and high degrees of stress, often quit their jobs to seek better positions. The annual turnover rate averaged 40 percent! One 85-year-old widow with severe disabilities said if her home care worker had left it would have been a disaster, since it takes months and continuity to build up the kind of trust and technique to reduce fear and help someone heal. Her health care worker was pleased that she would now get training to help clients who had Alzheimer's and other debilitating diseases.

The valuation of home health care work, as we saw in our earlier account of Joan, truly is a story of commonality of interests: It provides the home health care worker with a decent livelihood and respect, and it provides genuine care giving to those in our society who need it. Like the Norsk effort, the success of the campaign to organize home care workers depended on building on jointly recognized interests: The disability movement recognized the value of a stable, well-trained workforce; the government recognized that good home care programs save millions of dollars by providing an alternative to more costly hospital or nursing home care; and the home care workers recognized the significance of organizing for their working dignity.

❖ ❖ ❖

Other signs of hope are the small but important statements by public leaders that we need to reorganize work so that parents have more time to care for their children's needs. Thomas M. Menino, mayor of Boston and cochair of the United States Conference of Mayors' Task Force on Public Schools, recently called upon businesses to allow parents to take up to a half-day's leave each month to attend teacher conferences and other school meetings. He asked businesses to think about the significance of permitting parents to have more time to participate in their children's education. It would be beneficial not just for the parents but also, by strengthening families and raising educational outcomes, would help the larger community and businesses as well.

Menino's call reflects other national efforts to have businesses think beyond the usual bottom line and give people—parents, grandparents, and other adult mentors—time off from work to invest in children's educational needs. A call for a First Day of School Holiday, for example, is responding to research that demonstrates that parental involvement is the single most accurate predictor of a child's academic success.[16] Employers give parental involvement a boost by making the first day of school a paid or unpaid holiday. Positive school, family, and work relationships are launched each year that have both symbolic and concrete results. In 1997, First Day was launched in Vermont with 11 schools and 124 area employers, and by 2000 there were nearly 2,000 schools nationwide and several U.S. military bases abroad participating.

A third sign of hope is the notable movement for paid family medical leave. The United States is the only advanced industrialized country in the world that does not have any national form of paid family leave. In an age when dual-income or single-parent families are the norm, to not have a coherent national policy for paid family leave is irresponsible and damaging for the well-being of our families, our communities, and our country.

Today in America even moderately priced child care is beyond the means of many working families. Weekly rates average from $135 for an infant to $110 for children age three to twelve. For people in our country on core hourly wages, such costs exceed half of their gross income. If parents are working other than 9 to 5 days—on night or swing shifts—most often there are no child care centers open to provide care.

And all of us who have been parents are faced with days and even weeks of needing to care for sick children or elderly parents. Typically, parents either frantically scramble to decide which parent can most afford to stay home or search for a possible neighbor or friend to be a substitute.

More and more of us are attending to the needs of our aging parents, transporting them to health appointments and giving them necessary personal assistance. By the year 2030 one out of five people will be age 65 or older in the United States and already more than one quarter of us are providing care for a chronically ill or aged family member. Often we use up our own sick days, having to lie that we are ill, in order to stay home to be a caring parent or take care of our own parents. There is something very wrong with this picture of neglect and deception.

There have been some incremental signs of hope. Successful negotiations took place between Bloomingdale's flagship New York store and United Storeworkers Local 3 for an emergency child care benefit that would offer child care services at a state of the art center for a cost of $10 a day rather than the usual $135 a day. While that is a start, it does not address the core issues of children who are too sick to go to such a center or the fact that most children want to be home with a loving, familiar person when they are ill. Most parents, when they leave a sick child behind, have left worried hearts and minds at home as well.

❖　❖　❖

We have had unpaid family medical leave since 1994, and approximately 12 percent of those eligible have taken it so far, mostly women from large firms. But the current policy restrictions leave out 40 percent of the workforce—those in smaller companies, those who have not been in their jobs for the required period, and those who are in the nonstandard jobs where one out of four workers work today.

What do these limitations show us? If women, who still shoulder most of the care-giving responsibilities, were to cease taking on this task, we would be in terrible trouble. But the costs for women to continue carrying the dual burdens of paid and unpaid labor are very real—demonstrated in part by the physical and mental stresses for the women themselves. Men who have taken on such dual roles also face burnout. Even in families where there is some sharing of the work and family responsibilities, according to Sloan Foundation President Ralph Gomory, there are three jobs and two people.[17] Current institutional arrangements are woefully insufficient, and the managed care policies of the health care system have only made matters worse for many families in our nation. Therefore we need to change the institutions that address our dependent care needs—for our children, elders, and partners.

One way we can ensure care giving for all is to move to a universal system of paid leave, where people are encouraged by their workplaces to take the time out to be with those they are caring for and not have to worry that by doing so they are putting their livelihoods in jeopardy or undermining their value to the employer. The National Partnership for Family Leave Income Network is organizing people across boundaries—from business, labor, local community, and religious groups, men and women—to support the effort to create a viable family and medical leave program for our nation.[18]

What is at stake is the way we live in our society. Are we going to live in a culture where care giving is valued, or will we continue to devalue caring so that business can proceed as usual? Without a nation committed to care we will never be able to say: Yes, we can work and have a life.

Connecting Growth to Economic Security

The global economy has produced incredible growth and wealth. We need to ask: Growth by whom, for whom? Will this great accumulation of wealth move all of us closer to a decent livelihood and security or will it cause us to move toward greater impoverishment of our human dignity?

Big transnational corporations such as Exxon, Ford Motors, Mitsubishi, Royal Dutch/Shell, and Wal-Mart in 1997 had sales greater than the gross national products of entire nations such as the Philippines, Israel, Columbia, and Venezuela. The world gross national product at the turn to the twenty-first century was about $40 trillion a year, with offshore production by the multinational corporations—what their foreign subsidiaries and affiliates produce in countries other than the home base—accounting for about $6 trillion of that amount.

The most significant change for Americans is the dramatic speed of the internationalization of the American economy. Thirty years ago the American economy was still largely self-contained. International trade was under 10 percent of our GNP, with exports under 3 percent. But one generation later, there has been a tripling of international transactions, and such trade constitutes over 30 percent of our wealth.

The strengths of globalization have been tied to economic implications of the technological explosion, especially in information technology. During the past two decades, the global network of computers, telephones, and televisions has increased its information carrying capacity a million times over.[19] Computing power doubles every 18 months or so. Today's $2,000 laptop computer is many more times powerful than a $10 million mainframe computer of the mid-1950s. Twenty-five years ago only 50,000 computers existed in the whole world. Today there are at least 140 million, and that number does not count the computer chips inside cars, washing machines, or talking greeting cards.

With all these advances there have also been grave inequities. The wealthiest 20 percent of the world's population control 86 percent of the globe's domestic product, while the poorest 20 percent control just 1 percent.[20] During the great economic boom of the 1990s, the richest 200 people in the world doubled their net worth to $1 trillion, more than the gross national products of Canada, Belgium, Spain, South Korea, Brazil, or Russia. And on the technology front, the wealthiest 20 percent of the population controlled 74 percent of all telephone lines. There were more computers in the United States than in the entire rest of the world.

Within our own country the economic growth has had uneven effects. Real income and wage levels have stagnated for the last 20 years. One out of four children in the United States lives in poverty. Race and gender remain prime factors in economic inequities for blacks and Hispanics. For example, in the first quarter of 2000, the unemployment rates for blacks and Hispanics were 7.8 percent and 5.9 percent respectively, whereas the unemployment rate for whites was only 3.5 percent. Women still only earn 72 cents to each dollar men earn.

Even those who have employment in this country are anxious about their long-range economic security. We saw how Dan, the biotech accountant, was worried about the security of his children and elderly parents despite his good job, and how Joan, the home health care worker, worried about her lack of pension for her old age. Our younger generation, often in nonstandard temp and consultant jobs or hopscotching from firm to firm, wonder how they can compose some safety nets of security along their life course.

We are left with the daunting question of, how can we ensure that the gains of the global economy can be shared? In this economic age, how can *all* of us—those of us in the United States joining those outside our nation—have work and a life, that provide security and dignity?

There are signs of hope that offer examples of people taking this question seriously and with conviction. There were signs of hope in the interface between the World Trade Organization members and the fair trade movement members, who saw globalization as igniting a race to the bottom rather than a lifting of fortune. The movement's members believe fair trade policy would

lift working conditions in developing countries instead of negatively affecting wages for lower-skilled workers. Members of the
World Bank are increasingly moving toward a call to forgive the
debts of the most impoverished countries.

Close to home, the links between job losses in manufacturing
regions of the United States and working conditions in developing
countries have been unclear to most Americans. Manufacturing
workers here have usually felt anger toward foreign low-skilled
workers for taking away their jobs. A recent documentary film,
From the Mountain to the Maquiladoras, traces a new consciousness
among American female factory workers. The women from Tennessee go to Mexico to see for themselves where their jobs went when
their plant was shut down.[21] When they get there, they see the
shacks next to open sewers where their counterparts live; these
shacks are made from the cardboard boxes that had been used to
ship the factory equipment from Tennessee to Mexico. And the
women from America then realize that their interests are not just
about their own jobs but also about the quality of jobs for the
Mexican women. This people-to-people connection is a story of
consciousness raising in America, of how our fortunes are connected to the fortunes of others in the global economy. It puts a
human face on the global economy. It is one of the first steps in
moving toward fundamental social change and, thus, an important
moment of hope.

Signs of hope also exist in the corporate world. There have been
efforts to establish principles of global responsibility for corporations to correspond to the efforts of local, national, and international nongovernmental organizations to reduce economic
inequality. While an early United Nations attempt to create a global
code of conduct for transnational corporations failed, other codes
developed in the last 15 years are viable today.[22] Among those that
have been effective and can be used as models in the future are the

South African Council of Churches Code of Business Conduct, which calls for investments that will help build a just postapartheid economy, and the CERES Principles that address company responsibilities for the environment. In addition, the MacBride principles, proposed in 1984 under the auspices of Nobel Peace Prize–winner and Amnesty International cofounder Sean MacBride, are a set of nine equal opportunity measures aimed at overcoming religious discrimination in employment in Northern Ireland. U.S. corporations, which account for about 6 percent of employment in companies in Northern Ireland, have become the main lever of strong fair-employment policies in the region.[23]

In the last few years, more and more conversations have taken place that bring together shareholders, corporations, religious groups, and local community organizations. These discussions have led to a number of companies' adoption of guidelines for their own firms and their contractors. Among the principles that have been asserted are crafting new relationships between corporations and local communities that aim toward sustainable economic development. Such development would emphasize participatory structures to build equitable, long-term visions for production and growth. Special attention would be given to meeting the basic needs of people who are living on the economic margins.

A number of business leaders present the case of why CEOs should care about corporate responsibility. For example, Edward McCracken, chairman and CEO of Silicon Computer Graphics Systems, states that information age businesses should care about community responsibility because, more than ever, they rely on partnerships to do things quickly and competitively in the global economy.[24] In the interests of their own businesses they need to create an attractive community package to attract the best people, which means offering a good quality of life to their workers. Businesses, therefore, should invest in developing world-class education and health systems in the community for their workers. This new breed of "civic entrepreneurs" fosters links between corporations and community sectors because these links produce collaborative advantages of regional resiliency and long-term development that are good for business. Workers who have a life, a good quality of life, are understood to be essential for a healthy future economy.

The people of Norsk Hydro learned that they have a more productive economy when people are satisfied. The managers joined employees in making changes not just to do good, but also because it made economic sense. Anita Roddick is an entrepreneur who helped launch the international firm Body Shop. She sees an inextricable link between the performance of her business and organizing work to support family and community: "While corporate philanthropy is important, no amount a company gives at the end of the year can impact on the community in the same way that changes in the way it runs its business can."[25] For Roddick, dignity at work and economic productivity go hand in hand.

❖ ❖ ❖

The time has come to move beyond the constraint of bottom-line thinking. For the sake of individual health, for the sake of family security, and for the sake of sustaining communities and the growth of democracy, we need to balance the profit-driven forces of the current market paradigm with practices and policies that ensure the common good. We can feel and see that all is not well with business as usual. A world without dignity is an unhealthy world.

For individuals, work is where we spend much of our lifetime and where we fulfill many of our capacities.[26] Having dignity at work as the valid measure for our daily labors would replace the present bottom line that depends on calculating people as things. For each of us, dignity at work rests on the three pillars of achieving adequate livelihood, self respect, and social responsibility through making a difference.

As individuals, gender role changes offer a significant opportunity to transform the way we integrate care-giving responsibilities and work. The desire and expectation of young men to become equal partners with women in care-giving responsibilities would create a new paradigm for our society. Moreover, equality in the workplace depends on the attainment of equality in the home.

For families, we need to assure that economic growth translates to right livelihood within our nation and abroad. Dual-income and single-parent households, families in America and families in the poorest countries of our world, need to be included as beneficiaries of technological advances and economic development. The reality of globalization is that we are bound together as never before in human history. The fate of our families is inexorably connected.

Our communities and the very future of democracy depend on the ability of citizens to have time to invest in the common good. If we continue to organize work so that no one has the time or energy to devote to civic activities, communities will falter and democracy will fail as a living process. Among our younger people, from ages 18 to 24, participation in national elections dropped from half in 1972 to less than a third in 1996.[27] If young people find the new-economy jobs, and are wedded to a 24/7 schedule that prevents them from having a life, they and our entire society will risk falling into a time of great imbalance, a time of vertigo and disintegration.

Common sense, however, tells us to pay attention to the signs of hope that point to the way ahead. This may be idealistic but it is not naïve. These signs already exist in our reality. We can link grass roots community efforts to unionization drives to corporate halls to national and international public policies.

The signs exist on the individual level and are intimately linked to the promise of institutional signs of hope. We can create the new forms of work that will give men and women the chance, even the encouragement, to live lives of fairness and balance. Efforts to overcome forced overtime, to promote portable benefits, to value care giving, to connect economic growth to economic security, are all out there today.

To move forward will take imagination and risk taking. Both have long been part of our nation's history and the history of the most noble human endeavors on our planet. It is time to reject complacency and cynicism and march toward dignity.

NOTES

NOTES FOR PREFACE

1. Amartya Sen, "Well-being, Agency, and Freedom: The Dewey Lectures 1984," *The Journal of Philosophy* 82, no.4 (1985): 211.
2. See William A. Parent, "Constitutional Values and Human Dignity," in *The Constitution of Rights: Human Dignity and American Values,* ed. Michael J. Meyer and William A. Parent (Ithaca: Cornell University Press, 1992).
3. Martin Luther King, Jr., "Letter from a Birmingham Jail," reprinted in *Civil Disobedience,* ed. Hugo Bedau (New York: Pegasus, 1969), 76-77.
4. Frederick Schauer, "Speaking of Dignity," in *The Constitution of Rights: Human Dignity and American Values,* ed. Michael J. Meyer and William A. Parent (Ithaca: Cornell University Press, 1992), 184.
5. During the 1980s and 1990s, I conducted interviews with unemployed women and women in the service-sector occupations as part of my research for the National Institute of Mental Health study, "The Private and Social Costs of Unemployment," Boston College; the National Science Foundation study, "Unemployment and the Lives of Children," Children's Hospital; the Villars Foundation study, "Older Women Workers," Wellesley College; and "The Meaning of Work in Women's Lives" study, Bunting Institute, Radcliffe College.

NOTES FOR CHAPTER ONE

1. The people described in this section were either part of research in Work, Family, and Community projects of the Radcliffe Public Policy Center or as noted in cited sources. Names have been changed to respect human subject confidentiality.
2. Cynthia Fuchs Epstein, "The Part-Time Solution and the Part-Time Problem," *Dissent* 46, no. 2 (1999): 96.
3. Nathan Cobb, "Upward Stability," *Boston Globe,* 31 October 1999, sec. A, p. 24.
4. Deborah Stone, "The Meaning and Value of Caring Work" (Cambridge: Radcliffe Public Policy Center, 1999).
5. Barbara Ehrenreich, "Maid to Order," *Harper's Magazine* 300 (April 2000): 63.
6. Martha Chen, "The Invisible Workforce: Women in the Informal Economy" (Cambridge: Radcliffe Public Policy Center, 1999).

7. Joshua D. Margolis, "Dignity in the Balance" (Ph.D. diss., Harvard University, 1997), 5. This is a groundbreaking, thorough discussion of the relationship of dignity to organizational theory.

8. Kant quoted in Michael J. Meyer, "Kant's Concept of Dignity and Modern Political Thought," *History of European Ideas* 8, no. 3 (1987): 319.

9. Michael Ignatieff, "Human Rights: The Midlife Crisis," *New York Book Review* 46, no. 9 (1999): 60.

10. I am influenced here by Amartya Sen's naming the freedom to achieve well-being "well-being freedom." See his full discussion, "Well-being, Agency, and Freedom, The Dewey Lectures 1984," *Journal of Philosophy* 82, no. 4 (1985).

11. Quoted in Derrick Z. Jackson, "The Loves of a Grandmother," *Boston Globe,* 14 January 2000, sec. A, p. 23.

12. Simone Petrement, *Simone Weil: A Life* (New York: Pantheon, 1976), 245.

13. Bitner in a private conversation with author in 1979 during the launch of the study "The Private and Social Costs of Unemployment."

14. Jonathon Mann, "A Remedy Required Around the World: Dignity," *Boston Globe,* 6 December 1998, sec. D, p. 3.

15. Melvin L. Kohn, "Unresolved Issues in the Relationship Between Work and Personality," in *The Nature of Work,* ed. Kai Erikson (New Haven: Yale University, 1990), 41.

16. Margolis, op cit., 126.

17. A series of nationwide focus groups on work, family, and community issues was conducted by the Radcliffe Public Policy Institute as part of the New Economic Equation Project that I directed from 1995 to 1997.

18. The term "hopscotching" was coined by the research team of Lotte Bailyn, Constance Perrin, Ann Bookman, Susan Eaton, Françoise Carré, Leslie Cintron, and myself as part of the "Professional Pathways: Work and Family in the Biotechnology Industry" study funded by the Alfred P. Sloan Foundation, Radcliffe Public Policy Center, 1997-1999.

NOTES FOR CHAPTER TWO

1. The group interviews in this section of the book were conducted as part of the New Economic Equation study of work, family, and community across the United States by researchers at the Radcliffe Public Policy Institute, which I directed from 1995 to 1997. It was supported in part by a grant from the Ford Foundation.

2. Tamara K. Hareven, *Family Time and Industrial Time* (New York: Cambridge University Press, 1982). Quotations from textile mill workers in this section are from this book, chapters 4 and 8.

3. Ibid., 207.

4. Ely Chinoy, *Automobile Workers and the American Dream* (Garden City, N.Y.: Doubleday, 1955).

5. Ibid., 78.

6. Robert H. Guest, "Men and Machines," *Personnel* (May 1955).

7. Ibid., 126.

8. Martha May, "The Historical Problem of the Family Wage: The Ford Motor Company and the Five-Dollar Day," in *Families and Work,* ed. Naomi Gerstel and Harriet Engel (Philadelphia: Temple University Press: 1987).

9. Ibid., 113.

10. Allan Carlson, *Family Questions: Reflections on the American Social Crisis* (New Brunswick, N.J.: Transaction Books, 1988), 144.

11. Ibid.

12. Randall Tobias, "Global Transformations: Lessons for American Businesses" (transcript of 1998 Whitman Series on the New Global Economy lecture, Radcliffe Public Policy Center, 1998).

13. Deborah Stone, "The Meaning and Value of Caring Work" (Cambridge: Radcliffe Public Policy Center, 1999).

14. A group interview that was conducted as part of the New Economic Equation study, op. cit.

15. Ibid.

16. "Urban Institute National Survey of American Families," in *Snapshots of American Families Health Insurance Coverage,* ed. Niall Brennan, John Holahan, and Genevieve Kenny (Washington, D.C.: Urban Institute, 1998).

17. Harvard Joint Center for Housing Studies, reprinted in *Boston Globe,* 21 June 1999, sec. A, p. 14.

18. Richard Freeman and Joel Rogers, *What Workers Want* (Ithaca: Cornell University Press, 1999), 13.

19. Marina Whitman, *New World, New Rules* (Cambridge: Harvard University Press, 1999), 65-66.

20. Ellen Goodman, "They're Very Rich, But Are They Smart," *Boston Globe,* 15 April 1999, sec. A, p. 25.

21. Frank Levy, *The New Dollars and Dreams: American Incomes and Economic Change* (New York: Russell Sage Foundation, 1998), 53.

22. Thomas Kochan, "The American Corporation as an Employer: Past, Present, and Future Possibilities," in *The American Corporation,* ed. C. Kaysen (Oxford: Oxford University Press, 1996), 250.

23. Quotes from focus group interviews conducted as part of the New Economic Equation study, op. cit.

24. David Hamburg in "New Economic Equation Report" (Cambridge: Radcliffe Public Policy Institute, 1996).

25. E. P. Thompson, "Time, Work-Discipline, and Industrial Capitalism," *Past and Present* 29 (1964): 61.

26. For a thorough and provocative discussion of the history of time and leisure, see Sebastian de Grazia, *Of Time, Work, and Leisure* (New York: Twentieth Century Fund, 1962).

27. See Benjamin K. Hunnicutt, *Kellogg's Six-Hour Day* (Philadelphia: Temple University Press, 1996) for a wonderful presentation of the Kellogg story.

28. Barry Bluestone and Stephen Rose, "Unraveling an Economic Enigma: Overworked and Underemployed," *American Prospect* 0, no. 31 (1997): 58-69.

29. Kathleen Christensen and Ralph Gomory, "Three Jobs, Two People," *Washington Post,* 2 June 1999, sec. A, p. 21.

30. Robert Heilbroner, *Twenty-first Century Capitalism* (New York: W.W. Norton, 1993), 58.

31. Adam Smith, *An Inquiry into the Nature and Causes of the Wealth of Nations* (New York: Modern Library, 1937), 734.

32. Adam Smith quoted in Heilbroner, op. cit., 54.

33. Juliet Schor, "The Insidious Cycle of Work and Spend," in *The Consumer Society,* ed. N. Goodwin, F. Ackerman, and D. Kiron (Washington, D.C.: Island Press, 1997), 47.

34. Ibid.

35. David Shi, *The Simple Life: Plain Living and High Thinking in American Culture* (New York: Oxford University Press, 1985), 13.
36. John Kenneth Galbraith, "The Unfinished Business of the Century," *Boston Globe,* 12 July 1999, sec. A, p. 11.
37. Heilbroner, op. cit., 110.
38. Margaret M. Quinn and Eva Buiatti, "Women Changing the Times," *New Solutions Winter* (1991), 48-56.
39. E. F. Schumacher, *Small is Beautiful: A Study of Economics as if People Mattered* (London: Blond and Briggs, 1973).
40. Scott and Helen Nearing, *Living the Good Life: How to Live Sanely and Simply in a Troubled World* (New York: Schocken Books, 1970), vii.
41. Walter and Juanita Nelson, "Pricing Green Beans," *Massachusetts Farm Bulletin* 108 (August 1980).

NOTES FOR CHAPTER THREE

1. Adam Smith, *An Inquiry into the Nature and Causes of the Wealth of Nations* (New York: Modern Library, 1937), 734.
2. Peter Drucker, *Concept of the Corporation* (New York: New American Library, 1983), 152.
3. Sara Lawrence-Lightfoot, *Respect: An Exploration* (Reading, Mass.: Perseus Books, 1999), 9.
4. Martin Buber, *I and Thou* (New York: Touchstone, 1996).
5. Judith Jordan, "A Relational Perspective on Self-Esteem" (Wellesley: Center for Research on Women at Wellesley College, 1994).
6. Jean Baker Miller and Irene Pierce Stiver, *The Healing Connection: How Women Form Relationships in Therapy and in Life* (Boston: Beacon Press, 1997), 46.
7. Mihaly Csikszentmihalyi, *Finding Flow: The Psychology of Engagement with Everyday Life* (New York: Basic Books, 1997), 58.
8. Nancy C. Morse and Robert S. Weiss, "The Function and Memory of Work and the Job," *American Sociological Review* 20, no. 2 (1955).
9. Jonathan Cobb and Richard Sennett, *The Hidden Injuries of Class* (New York: Norton, 1993), 92.
10. Phillipe Bourgois, *In Search of Respect: Selling Crack in El Barrio* (New York: Cambridge University Press, 1995), 143-44.
11. Ibid.
12. Suzanne Gordon, *Life Support: Three Nurses on the front Lines* (Boston: Little Brown and Company, 1997), 45.
13. From Katherine Newman interviews with me in March 1999 and from her award-winning book, *No Shame in My Game: The Working Poor in the Inner City* (New York: Knopf and Russell Sage Foundation, 1999). To add an interesting global perspective, my research assistant Chiwen Bao noted that in East Asia workers are generally proud to work at McDonald's or Kentucky Fried Chicken establishments because they see themselves as part of something global and embedded in American values and culture.
14. Ann Barnard and Katherine Tong, "The Doctor is Out," *Boston Globe,* 9 July 2000, sec. A, p. 18.
15. Cynthia Fuchs Epstein, et al., *The Part-Time Paradox: Time Norms, Professional Lives, Family, and Gender* (New York: Routeledge, 1999), 84.
16. Ibid., 85.

17. Jonathan Cobb and Richard Sennett, op. cit., 83.

18. Paula Rayman and Barry Bluestone, *Out of Work: The Consequences of Unemployment in the Hartford Aircraft Industry* (Washington, D.C.: National Institute of Mental Health, 1981).

19. Robert Merton. *Social Theory and Social Structure* (New York: Free Press, 1968).

20. Among the best studies on this subject are Robert Angell, *The Family Encounters the Depression* (New York: Charles Scribner's Sons, 1936); Mirra Komarovsky, *The Unemployed Man and His Family* (New York: Octagon Books, 1971); Ramsay Liem, "The Psychological Costs of Unemployment: A Comparison of Findings and Definitions," *Social Research* 54, no. 2 (1987); and Harry Maurer, *Not Working: An Oral History of the Unemployed* (New York: Holt, Rinehart, & Winston, 1979).

21. Marie Jahoda, et al., *Marienthal: The Sociography of an Unemployed Community* (Chicago: Atherton, 1971).

22. Paula Rayman, "Unemployment and Family Life: The Meaning for Children" (paper presented at Economic and Distress and Families Symposium, University of Dayton Conference on Family, October 1985).

23. Katherine Newman, *Falling From Grace: Downward Mobility in the Age of Affluence* (Berkeley: University of California Press, 1999).

24. William Julius Wilson, *When Work Disappears: The World of the New Urban Poor* (New York: Knopf, 1996), 160.

25. For a comprehensive listing of historical studies from the depression era in the United States as well as studies from the post-World War II period, see the extensive bibliography listed in Rayman and Bluestone, op. cit.

26. Deborah Stone, "The Meaning and Value of Caring Work" (Cambridge: Radcliffe Public Policy Center, 1999).

27. Paula Rayman, "Women and Employment," *Social Research* 54, no. 2 (1987).

NOTES FOR CHAPTER FOUR

1. The people described in this section were either part of research in Work, Family, and Community projects of the Radcliffe Public Policy Center or encountered in cited sources. Names have been changed to respect human subject confidentiality.

2. William Sullivan, *Work and Integrity* (New York: Harper Business, 1995), 16.

3. Anne Colby et al., ed., *Competence and Character Through Life* (Chicago: University of Chicago Press, 1998).

4. John Demos, *A Little Commonwealth* (New York: Oxford University Press, 1970).

5. Thomas Jefferson, *The Complete Jefferson,* ed. Saul K. Padover (New York: Duell, Sloan, and Pearce, 1943), 676.

6. Alexis de Tocqueville, *Democracy In America,* trans. George Lawrence, ed. J.P. Mayer (New York: Doubleday, Anchor Books, 1969), 508.

7. Quoted in Robert Heilbroner, "The Paradox of Progress: Decline and Decay in *Wealth of Nations,*" in *Essays on Adam Smith,* ed. Andrew Skinner and Thomas Wilson (Oxford: Clarendon Press, 1975), 524-39.

8. United States Kerner Commission, *Report of the National Advisory Commission on Civil Disorders* (New York: Bantam Books, 1968).

9. For two different but compatible perspectives on this theme, see Juliet Schor, The *Overworked American: The Unexpected Decline of Leisure* (New York: Basic

Books, 1991) and Robert Kuttner, *Everything for Sale: The Virtues and Limits of Markets* (New York: Alfred A. Knopf, 1997).

10. Robert Merton, *Social Theory and Social Structure* (New York: Free Press, 1968), 432.

11. Richard Knox, "Trailblazing Boston Doctors Union at Core of Pivotal Case," *Boston Globe,* 14 November 1999, sec. A, p. 1.

12. Brigid O'Farrell and Joyce Kornbluh, ed., *Rocking the Boat: Union Women's Voices, 1915-1975* (New Brunswick: Rutgers University Press, 1996).

13. Martin Buber, *I and Thou* (New York: Touchstone, 1996).

14. Avrahan Shapira, "Work," in *Contemporary Jewish Religious Thought,* ed. Arthur A. Cohen and Paul Mendes-Flohr (New York: Free Press, 1988).

15. Paula Rayman, *The Kibbutz Community and Nation Building* (Princeton: Princeton University Press, 1981.

16. John Russo and Brian R. Corbin, "Labor and the Catholic Church: Opportunities for Coalitions," *Working USA* 3, no. 2 (1999), 81.

17. Catholic Church, *Economic Justice for All: Pastoral Letter on Catholic Social Teaching and the U.S. Economy* (Washington, D.C.: National Conference of Catholic Bishops, 1986), 3.

18. Ibid., 13.

19. "Work and Leisure," *Blackwell Encyclopedia of Modern Christian Thought,* ed. Alister McGrath (Oxford: Blackwell Publishers, 1993).

20. Martin Luther King, Jr., *A Testament of Hope,* ed. James Melvin Washington (San Francisco: Harper and Row, 1986), 247.

21. Ibid., 248.

22. *The Holy Qur'an* 8:41, trans. M.H. Shakir (New York: Tahrike Tarsile Qur'an, Inc., 1983).

23. For more information on the Four Noble Truths and the Eightfold Path, refer to http://buddhism.about.com/religion/buddhism/blbud101.htm

24. E-mail exchange with research partner Michelle G. Lee. For more background on the *kyeh* system in America, see Eui Young Yu, ed., *Black-Korean Encounter: Toward Understanding and Alliance* (Los Angeles: Regina Books, 1994).

25. From my interviews with Chinese garment workers in collaboration with the Chinese Progressive Association and the Older Women's Advocacy Center, Wellesely College, 1988.

26. Michael Maccoby and Katherine Terzi, "Character and Work in America," in *Exploring Contradictions,* ed. Philip Brenner, Robert Borosage, and Bethany Weidner (New York: David McKay Company, 1974), 157.

27. Katherine Newman, *Falling from Grace: Downward Mobility in the Age of Affluence* (Berkley: University of California Press, 1999). Her study of the Singer Sewing Machine workers is a classic accounting of the costs of unemployment, in the spirit of *Marienthal* which was done fifty years earlier.

28. Deborah Stone, "The Meaning and Value of Caring Work" (Cambridge: Radcliffe Public Policy Center, 1999).

29. Ibid., 5.

30. Ibid., 8.

31. Paula Rayman and Belle Brett, *Pathways for Women in the Sciences* (Wellesley: Wellesley College Center for Research on Women, 1993).

32. M. Whitebook and D. Bellm, *Taking on Turnover* (Washington, D.C.: Center for the Childcare Workforce, 1999).

33. Stephanie Coontz, *The Way We Really Are* (New York: Basic Books, 1997).

34. Kristen Gore, "Telemommies" (Senior honors thesis in Social Studies, Harvard University, 1998).

35. From a conversation with Katherine Newman in March 1998 and from her book *Falling from Grace*, op. cit., chapter 5. Also from an interview I conducted with a participant in a focus group on generation X in spring 1999. The participant was a daughter of one of the air traffic controllers laid off in 1981 and offered vivid recollections of the effects of the strike and layoff for her own life, her family, and her community.

36. Françoise Carré, Paula Rayman, et al., "Professional Pathways: Examining Work, Family, and Community in the Biotechnology Industry," executive summary (Cambridge, Radcliffe Public Policy Center, 1999).

37. Robert Bellah, ed., *Habits of the Heart: Individualism and Commitment in American Life* (Berkeley: University of California Press, 1985) and Robert Wuthnow, *Acts of Compassion: Caring for Others and Helping Ourselves* (Princeton: Princeton University Press, 1991).

38. For the various, often disagreeing, perspectives reviewed here, see Robert D. Putnam, *Bowling Alone: Civic Disengagement in America* (New York: Simon & Schuster, 2000); Theda Skocpol, "Unraveling from Above," in *Ticking Time Bombs*, ed. Robert Kuttner (New York: New York Press, 1996); Everett Carll Ladd, *The Ladd Report* (New York: Free Press, 1999); Robert Wuthnow, *Loose Connections: Journey Together in America's Fragmental Communities* (Cambridge: Harvard University Press, 1998); Francis Fukuyama, *The Great Disruption: Human Nature and the Reconstruction of Social Order* (New York: Free Press, 1999). See also an excellent review of the subject in D.W. Miller, "Perhaps We Bowl Alone, But Does It Really Matter?" *The Chronicle of Higher Education*, 16 July 1999, pp. A 16-17.

NOTES FOR CHAPTER FIVE

1. This chapter is largely based on the research project *Professional Pathways: Examining Work, Family, and Community in the Biotechnology Industry* (Cambridge: Radcliffe Public Policy Center, 1999), funded by the Alfred P. Sloan Foundation. The research team included myself and Françoise Carré as principal investigators; Lotte Bailyn, Ann Bookman, and Constance Perin as study directors; Susan Eaton as senior research associate; and Leslie Cintron as research associate.

2. To make this cooperation viable, a number of ground rules were established during the early negotiations. Individual sites were to be given code names and used instead of the real names by all researchers. Identities of individual workers, during interviews and focus groups, were to be kept confidential. And the human subject guidelines marking all such research at Harvard University were to be strictly adhered to by all research team members. We agreed at the end of the study to share basic findings back to the study sites.

3. Since field research ended, the three companies have continued to undergo change. Prima acquired another small biotech firm, and the current pipeline of maturing products includes both vaccines and immuno-therapeutics. Segunda is collaborating with seven corporate partners including three of the world's four largest vaccine manufacturers to develop new products for the treatment of infectious diseases and cancers. Tertia underwent a merger to form a new publicly traded division of its original parent company. The transaction will be

completed in late 2000. The new division will have approximately 1,300 employees, six dedicated manufacturing facilities, and global clinical and regulatory capabilities.

NOTES FOR CHAPTER SIX

1. The research for this chapter is based on a case study conducted by the Radcliffe Public Policy Center, "The Radcliffe-Fleet Project: Creating Work and Life Integration Solutions" (Cambridge: Radcliffe Public Policy Institute, 1998). The research team included Lotte Bailyn and myself as co-principal investigators, with Maureen Harvey, Robert Kum, Robert Read, Françoise Carré, Jillian Dickert, Pamela Joshi, and Alina Martinez. Funding came from Fleet Financial, and the research was greatly aided by the interest and support of many Fleet managers and employees. There is a published executive summary of the full research report.

2. William Atkinson, "Employee Fatigue," *Management Review* 88 (October 1999).

3. For a report on both sites, see "The Radcliffe-Fleet Project: Creating Work and Life Integration Solutions."

4. There is a phenomenon known in social science as the Hawthorne Effect whereby the intervention by itself causes the situation to change. In a sense, this happened to some degree at the banks, as the research team—just by raising the possibility for employees to have more say in their work organization—altered their expectations, their hopes, and their work environment. For a fuller discussion of the Hawthorne Effect, see *Encyclopedia of Psychology* (Guilford, Conn.: DPG Reference Pub., 1981).

NOTES FOR CHAPTER SEVEN

1. Stephen Greenhouse, "In Biggest Drive Since 1937, Union Gains a Victory," *New York Times,* 26 Feb. 1999, sec. A, p. 1.

2. Radcliffe Public Policy Center, "Work and Life 2000: An Employer's Guide" (Cambridge: Radcliffe Public Policy Institute, 1998). Also see "Rating the 100," *Working Mother,* October 2000, pp. 75-83.

3. This experiment is part of the Radcliffe/Health and Human Services project, begun in 1999 and due for completion in 2001, led by Cynthia Costello, Senior Researcher of the Radcliffe Public Policy Center.

4. Renana Jhabuala, "Excluding the Majority: Workers, Producers, and Categories of Employment," SEWA, Ahmedabad, India.

5. The story of Norsk Hydro first came to my attention, at the invitation of Professor Lotte Bailyn, when I met Ragnhild Sohlberg, vice president of External Relations and Special Projects of the company, at a 1998 MIT seminar on the future of work. Since that time I have had many conversations with Sohlberg about her company and the Hydroflex project. An excellent article on the experiment appeared in *Fast Company,* written by Charles Fishman, July-August 1999 issue. Some of the facts about the experiment are drawn from this article.

6. The study "Life's Work: Generational Attitudes Toward Work and Life Integration" was conducted by the Radcliffe Public Policy Center with Harris Interac-

tive, Inc. and sponsored by FleetBoston Financial. An executive summary was published by the Radcliffe Public Policy Center, Cambridge, Mass., 2000.

7. A number of recent publications have addressed the care crisis in America including Mona Harrington, *Care and Equality: Inventing a New Family Politics* (New York: Alfred A Knopf, 1999), and Deborah Stone, "Why We Need a Care Movement," *The Nation* 270, no. 10 (2000).

8. Helen Epstein, "Life and Death on the Social Ladder," *New York Review of Books* VXLV, No. 12 (1998): 26-30. I would like to thank Richard Freeman for this citation.

9. Lisa Dodson, *Don't Call Us Out of Name: The Untold Lives of Women and Girls in Poor America* (Boston: Beacon Press, 1999).

10. Glen Johnson, "Flight Crew Fatigue Raised in Grievance," *Boston Globe,* 26 June 1999, sec. A, p. 6.

11. ILO study by John Doohan, "Working Longer, Working Better?" *World of Work* 31 (1999).

12. Suzanne Gordon and Steve Early, "Bad Blood at St. Vincent," *Boston Globe,* 12 April 2000, editorial page.

13. "Too Many Hours," *Boston Globe,* 7 April 2000, editorial page.

14. Kenneth J. Moynihan, "Why People Side with Nurses in Dispute," (Worcester) *Telegram and Gazette,* 22 March 2000, sec. A, p. 13.

15. *Labor News for Working Families* VIII, no. 1 (1999): 1. Lonnie M. Golden, "Saying No to the Boss," *Boston Globe,* 6 September 1998, sec. C, p. 1.

16. The First Day campaign is one example that calls on businesses to shut down or give time off on the first day of the school year.

17. Lecture by Ralph Gomory, "Work and Family: Inherent Conflict," Gender and Inquiry Symposium, Radcliffe Institute of Advanced Study, October 13, 2000.

18. See National Partnership for Family-Medical Leave Network, Washington, D.C.

19. Statistics in this paragraph are from "The Hitchhikers Guide to Cybernomics," *The Economist,* 28 September 1996.

20. Figures in this paragraph are from the tenth annual United Nations Development Program's *Human Development Report,* United Nations, New York, July 1999.

21. Njoki Njorge Njehu, in "Free Trade and the 'Starving Child Defense': A Forum." *The Nation* 270, no. 16 (2000): 27.

22. See David Schilling and Ruth Rosenbaum, "Principles for Global Corporate Responsibility," *Business and Society Review,* no. 94 (1995): 55-56, for a full discussion.

23. Angela Hegarty, "Examining Equality: The Fair Employment Act of 1989 and Its Review," *Web Journal of Current Legal Issues,* Blackstone Press Ltd., 1995.

24. Douglas Henton, John Melville, and Kimberly Walesh, *Grassroots Leaders for a New Economy* (San Francisco: Jossey-Bass, 1997).

25. Anita Roddick, "Reflections on Community, Work and Family Linkages" *Community, Work, and Family* 1, no. 1, (1998): 11.

26. Daniel Bell, *The Cultural Contradictions of Capitalism* (New York: Basic Books, 1976). Bell has written eloquently for a long time on the need to create a change in our economic consciousness.

27. Lynne Casper and Loretta Bass, "Voting and Registration in the Election of November 1996" *Current Population Survey,* July 1998.

BIBLIOGRAPHY

Angell, R. C. *The Family Encounters the Depression*. New York: Charles Scribner's Sons, 1936.

Atkinson, W. "Employee Fatigue." *Management Review* 88 (October 1999).

Babson, J. "Study: Homeownership Soars but Poor Can't Afford Rent." *Boston Globe*. 21 June 1999, A14.

Bailyn, L. "Autonomy in the Industrial R&D Lab." *Human Resource Management* 24, no. 2 (1989): 129-46.

Bailyn, L., P. Rayman et al. Radcliffe-Fleet Project: Creating Work and Life Integration Solutions. Radcliffe Public Policy Center, Cambridge, Mass., 1998.

Bakke, E. W. *The Unemployed Worker: A Study of the Task of Making a Living Without a Job*. New Haven: Yale University Press, 1940.

Barnard, A., and K. Tong. "The Doctor Is Out." *Boston Globe*. 9 July 2000, A18.

Bell, D. *The Cultural Contradictions of Capitalism*. New York: Basic Books, 1976.

Bellah, R., ed. *Habits of the Heart: Individualism and Commitment in American Life*. Berkeley: University of California Press, 1985.

Belle, D. *Lives in Stress: Women and Depression*. Beverly Hills: Sage Publications, 1982.

Berry, W. *The Unsettling of America: Culture and Agriculture*. San Francisco: Sierra Club Books, 1996.

Blackwell Encyclopedia of Modern Christian Thought. ed. Alister McGrath. Oxford: Blackwell Publishers, 1993.

Bluestone, B., and S. Rose. "Unraveling an Economic Enigma: Overworked and Underemployed." *American Prospect* 0, no. 31 (1997): 58-69.

Bourgois, P. I. *In Search of Respect: Selling Crack in El Barrio*. New York: Cambridge University Press, 1995.

Brenner, M. H. *Mental Illness and the Economy*. Cambridge: Harvard University Press, 1973.

Buber, M. *I and Thou*. New York: Touchstone, 1996.

Carlson, A. *Family Questions: Reflections on the American Social Crisis*. New Brunswick, N.J.: Transaction Books, 1988.

Carré, F., P. Rayman et al. "Professional Pathways: Examining Work, Family, and Community in the Biotechnology Industry." Radcliffe Public Policy Center, Cambridge, Mass., 1999.

Catholic Church and National Conference of Catholic Bishops. *Economic Justice for All: Pastoral Letter on Catholic Social Teaching and the U.S. Economy.* U.S. Catholic Conference, Washington, D.C., 1986.

Chen, M. "The Invisible Workforce: Women in the Informal Economy." Radcliffe Public Policy Center, Cambridge, Mass., 1999.

Chinoy, E. *Automobile Workers and the American Dream.* Garden City, N.Y.: Doubleday, 1955.

Christensen, K. and R. Gomory. "Three Jobs, Two People." *Washington Post.* 2 June 1999, A21.

Clague, E. and W. Powell. *Ten Thousand Out of Work.* Philadelphia: University of Pennsylvania Press, 1933.

Cobb, J., and R. Sennett. *The Hidden Injuries of Class.* New York: Norton, 1993.

Cobb, N. "Upward Stability." *Boston Globe.* 31 October 1999, A24.

Colby, A., J. James et al., eds. *Competence and Character Through Life.* Chicago: University of Chicago Press, 1998.

Coles, R. *Children of Crisis.* Boston: Little Brown, 1967.

Coontz, S. *The Way We Really Are.* New York: Basic Books, 1997.

Csikszentmihalyi, M. *Finding Flow: The Psychology of Engagement with Everyday Life.* New York: Basic Books, 1997.

Demos, J. *A Little Commonwealth.* New York: Oxford University Press, 1970.

Dodson, L. *Don't Call Us Out of Name: The Untold Lives of Women and Girls in Poor America.* Boston: Beacon Press, 1999.

Doohan, J. "Working Harder, Working Better?" *World of Work* 31 (1999).

Drucker, P. F. *Concept of the Corporation.* New York: New American Library, 1983.

Ehrenreich, B. "Maid to Order." *Harper's* 300 (April 2000).

Elder, J. Glen. *The Children of the Depression.* Chicago: University of Chicago, 1974.

Encyclopedia of Psychology. Guilford, Conn.: DPG Reference Pub., 1981.

Epstein, H. "Life and Death on the Social Ladder." *New York Review of Books* XLV, no. 12 (1998): 26-30.

Epstein, C. F., C. Seron et al. *The Part-time Paradox: Time Norms, Professional Lives, Family, and Gender.* New York: Routledge, 1999.

Epstein, C. F. "The Part-Time Solution and the Part-Time Problem." *Dissent* 46, no. 2 (1999).

Erikson, K., and S. P. Vallas, eds. *The Nature of Work: Sociological Perspectives.* American Sociological Association Presidential Series. New Haven: Yale University Press, 1990.

Faludi, S. *Stiffed: The Betrayal of the American Man.* New York: William Morrow and Co., 1999.

Fishman C. "The Way to Enough." *Fast Company.* July-August 1999.

Four Noble Truths and the Eightfold Path, About.com. (2000).

Freeman, R. B., and J. Rogers. *What Workers Want.* Ithaca: Cornell University Press, 1999.

Freud, S. *Civilization and Its Discontents.* New York: W. W. Norton, 1961.

Fukuyama, F. *The Great Disruption: Human Nature and the Reconstruction of Social Order.* New York: Free Press, 1999.

Galbraith, J. K. "The Unfinished Business of the Century." *Boston Globe.* 12 July 1999, A11.

Golden, L. "Saying 'No.'" *Boston Globe.* 6 September 1998, C1.

Goodman, E. "They're Very Rich But Are They Smart." *Boston Globe.* 15 April 1999, A25.

Gomory, R. "Work and Family: Inherent Conflict." Gender and Inquiry Symposium at Radcliffe Institute of Advanced Study, Cambridge, Mass., 13 October 2000.

Gordon, S. *Life Support: Three Nurses on the Front Line.* Boston: Little, Brown, and Company, 1997.

Gordon, S., and S. Early. "Bad Blood at St. Vincent." *Boston Globe.* 12 April 2000.

Gore, K. "Telemommies." Undergraduate thesis, Harvard University, 1998.

Grazia, S. d. *Of Time, Work, and Leisure.* New York: Twentieth Century Fund, 1962.

Greenhouse, S. "In Biggest Drive Since 1937, Union Gains a Victory." *New York Times.* 26 February 1999, A1.

Greider, W. *One World, Ready or Not: The Manic Logic of Global Capitalism.* New York: Simon & Schuster, 1997.

Guest, R. H. Men and Machines. *Personnel* (May 1955).

Guest, R. H. "Quality of Work Life-Learning from Tarrytown." *Harvard Business Review* 57, no. 4 (1979).

Hamburg, David. "New Economic Equation Report." Radcliffe Public Policy Institute, Cambridge, Mass., 1996.

Hareven, T. K. *Family Time and Industrial Time: The Relationship Between the Family and Work in a New England Industrial Community.* Cambridge: Cambridge University Press, 1982.

Harrington, M. *Care and Equity: Inventing a New Family Politics.* New York, Alfred A. Knopf, 1999.

Harvard Joint Center for Housing Studies. *Boston Globe*. 21 June 1999, A14.

Hegel, G. W. F. *Hegel's Philosophy of Right*. Oxford: Oxford University Press, 1967.

Heilbroner, R. "The Paradox of Progress: Decline and Decay in Wealth of Nations." In *Essays on Adam Smith,* eds. A. Skinner and T. Wilson. Oxford: Clarendon Press, 1975.

Heilbroner, R. L. *Twenty-first Century Capitalism*. New York: W.W. Norton, 1993.

Henton, D., J. Melville, et al. *Grassroots Leaders for a New Economy*. San Francisco: Jossey-Bass, 1997.

"Hitchhiker's Guide to Cybernomics." *The Economist,* 28 September 1996.

Hodson, R. "Dignity in the Workplace Under Participative Management: Alienation and Freedom Revisited." *American Sociological Review* 61, no. 5 (1996): 719-38.

Holy Qur'an. New York: Tahrike Tarsile Qur'an, Inc., 1983.

Hopkins, M., and J. L. Seglin. "Americans at Work." *Inc*. 19, no. 7 (1997): 77-85.

Horwitz, T. "These Growth Jobs are Dull, Dead-end, Sometimes Dangerous." *Wall Street Journal*. 1 December 1994, A1.

Hunnicutt, B. K. *Kellogg's Six-Hour Day*. Philadelphia: Temple University Press, 1996.

Ignatieff, M. "Human Rights: The Midlife Crisis." *New York Book Review* 46, no. 9 (1999): 58-62.

Jackson, D. Z. "The Loves of a Grandmother." *Boston Globe*. 14 January 2000, A23.

Jahoda, M., P. F. Lazarsfeld, et al. *Marienthal: The Sociography of an Unemployed Community*. Chicago: Atherton, 1971.

Jhabuala, R. "Excluding the Majority: Workers, Producers, and Categories of Employment." Ahmedabad, India, SEWA.

Johnson, G. "Flight Crew Fatigue Raised in Grievance." *Boston Globe*. 26 June 1999, A6.

Jordan, J. "A Relational Perspective on Self-Esteem," Center for Research on Women at Wellesley College, Wellesley, Mass., 1994.

King, Jr., M.L. *A Testament of Hope,* ed. J. M. Washington. San Francisco: Harper and Row, 1986.

King, Jr., M. L. "Letter from the Birmingham Jail." In *Civil Disobedience,* ed. H. Bedau. New York: Pegasus, 1969.

Knox, R. "Trailblazing Boston Doctors Union at Core of Pivotal Case." *Boston Globe*. 14 November 1999, A1.

Kochan, T. A. "The American Corporation as an Employer: Past, Present and Future Possibilities." In *The American Corporation Today,* eds. C. Kaysen. Oxford: Oxford University Press, 1996.

Kohn, M. L. "Unresolved Issues in the Relationship between Work and Personality." In *The Nature of Work*, eds. K. Erikson. New Haven: Yale University Press, 1990.

Kolnai, A. "Dignity." *Philosophy* 51, (1976): 251-71.

Komansky, D. H. *Principled Leadership*. Merrill Lynch Global Leadership Conference, 1995.

Komarovsky, M. *The Unemployed Man and His Family*. New York: Octagon Books, 1971.

Kuttner, R. *Everything for Sale: The Virtues and Limits of Markets*. New York: Alfred A. Knopf, 1997.

Labor News for Working Families 8, no. 1 (1999).

Ladd, E. C. *The Ladd Report*. New York: Free Press, 1999.

Lawrence-Lightfoot, S. *Respect: An Exploration*. Reading, Mass.: Perseus Books, 1999.

Levy, F. *The New Dollars and Dreams: American Incomes and Economic Change*. New York: Russell Sage Foundation, 1998.

Liem, R. "The Psychological Costs of Unemployment: A Comparison of Findings and Definitions." *Social Research* 54, no. 2 (1987).

Liem, R., and J. Liem. "Social Class and Mental Illness Remembered: The Role of Economic Stress and Social Support." *Journal of Health and Social Support* 19 (1978): 139-56.

"Life's Work: Generational Attitudes toward Work and Life Integration." Radcliffe Public Policy Center, Cambridge, Mass., 2000.

Maccoby, M., and Terzi, K. "Character and Work in America." In *Exploring Contradictions*, eds. P. Brenner, R. Borosage and B. Weidner. New York: David McKay Company, 1974.

Mann, J. "A Remedy Required Around the World: Dignity." *Boston Globe*. 6 December 1987, D3.

Margolis, J. "Dignity in the Balance." Ph.D. diss., Harvard University, 1997.

Maurer, H. *Not Working: An Oral History of the Unemployed*. New York: Holt, Rinehart, and Winston, 1979.

May, M. "The Historical Problem of the Family Wage: The Ford Motor Company and the Five-Dollar Day." In *Families and Work*, eds. N. Gerstel and H. Engel. Philadelphia: Temple University Press, 1987.

Melden, A. I. "Dignity, Worth, and Rights." In *The Constitution of Rights: Human Dignity and American Values*, eds. M. Meyer and W. A. Parent. Ithaca: Cornell University Press, 1992.

Merton, R. K. *Social Theory and Social Structure*. New York: Free Press, 1968.

Meyer, M. J. "Kant's Concept of Dignity and Modern Political Thought." *History of European Ideas* 8, no. 3 (1987): 319-32.

Miller, J. B., and I. P. Stiver. *The Healing Connection: How Women Form Relationships in Therapy and in Life.* Boston: Beacon Press, 1997.

Morse, N. C., and R. Weiss. "The Function and Memory of Work and the Job." *American Sociological Review* 20, no. 2 (1955).

Moynihan, K. J. "Why People Side with Nurses in Dispute." (Worcester) *Telegram and Gazette,* 22 March 2000, A13.

Nearing, H., and S. *Living the Good Life: How to Live Sanely and Simply in a Troubled World.* New York: Schocken Books, 1970.

Nelson, W., and J. "Pricing Green Beans." *Massachusetts Farm Bulletin* 108, 20 July 1980.

Newman, K. S. *No Shame in My Game: The Working Poor in the Inner City.* New York: Knopf and Russell Sage Foundation, 1999.

Newman, K. S. *Falling from Grace: Downward Mobility in the Age of Affluence.* Berkeley: University of California Press, 1999.

Njehu, N. N. in "Free Trade and the 'Starving Child Defense': A Forum." *The Nation* 270, no. 16 (2000): 27.

Nussbaum, M. "Nature, Function, and Capability: Aristotle on Political Distribution." *Oxford Studies in Ancient Philosophy, Supplement* (1988): 145-84.

O'Farrell, B., and J. Kornbluh, eds. *Rocking the Boat: Union Women's Voices, 1915-1975.* New Brunswick: Rutgers University Press, 1996.

Padover, S. K., ed. *The Complete Jefferson.* New York: Duell, Sloan, and Pearce, 1943.

Parent, W. A. "Constitutional Values and Human Dignity." In *The Constitution of Rights: Human Dignity and American Values,* eds. M. J. Meyer and W. A. Parent. Ithaca: Cornell University Press, 1992.

Petrement, S. *Simone Weil: A Life.* New York: Pantheon Books, 1976.

Putnam, R. D. *Bowling Alone: Civic Disengagement in America.* New York: Simon and Schuster, 2000.

Quinn, M. and E. Buiatti. "Women Changing the Times." *New Solutions* (Winter 1991): 48-56.

Radcliffe Public Policy Center. New Economic Equation. Cambridge, MA: Radcliffe College, 1997.

Rayman, P. *The Kibbutz Community and Nation Building.* Princeton: Princeton University Press, 1981.

Rayman, P. M., and B. Bluestone. *Out of Work: The Consequences of Unemployment in The Hartford Aircraft Industry.* Washington, D.C.: National Institute of Mental Health, 1981.

Rayman, P. "Unemployment and Family Life: The Meaning for Children." University of Dayton, Ohio, Conference on the Family, 1985.

Rayman, P. "Women and Unemployment." *Social Research* 54, no. 2 (1987).

Rayman, P. and B. Brett. *Pathways for Women in the Sciences.* Wellesley: Wellesley College Center for Research on Women, 1992.

Rollins, J. *Between Women: Domestics and Their Employers.* Philadelphia: Temple University Press, 1985.

Russo, J., and B. R. Corbin. "Labor and the Catholic Church: Opportunities for Coalition." *Working USA* 3, no. 2 (1999).

Schauer, F. "Speaking of Dignity." In *The Constitution of Rights: Human Dignity and American Values,* edited by M. J. Meyer and W. A. Parent. Ithaca: Cornell University Press, 1992.

Schilling, D. M., and R. Rosenbaum. "Principles for Global Corporate Responsibility." *Business and Society Review* 94 (Summer 1995): 55-56.

Schor, J. *The Overworked American: The Unexpected Decline of Leisure.* New York: Basic Books, 1991.

Schor, J. "The Insidious Cycle of Work and Spend." In *The Consumer Society,* eds. N. R. Goodwin, F. Ackerman, and D. Kiron. Washington, D.C.: Island Press, 1997.

Schumacher, E. F. *Small is Beautiful: A Study of Economics as if People Mattered.* London: Blond and Briggs, 1973.

Schumpeter, J. A. "The Present World Depression: A Tentative Diagnosis." Reprinted from *American Economic Review Supplement* XXI, No. 1 (1931):179-82.

Sen, A. "Well-being, Agency, and Freedom: The Dewey Lectures 1984." *Journal of Philosophy* 82, no. 4 (1985): 169-221.

Sennett, R., and J. Cobb. *The Hidden Injuries of Class.* New York: Norton, 1993.

Shapira, A. "Work." In *Contemporary Jewish Religious Thought,* eds. A. A. Cohen and P. Mendes-Flohr. New York: Free Press, 1988.

Shi, D. *The Simple Life: Plain Living and High Thinking in American Culture.* New York: Oxford University Press, 1985.

Skocpol, T. "Unraveling from Above." In *Ticking Time Bombs,* edited by R. Kuttner. New York: New York Press, 1996.

Smith, A. *An Inquiry into the Nature and Causes of the Wealth of Nations.* New York: Modern Library, 1937.

Stack, C. B. *All Our Kin: Strategies for Survival in a Black Community.* New York: Harper & Row, 1975.

Stone, D. "The Meaning and Value of Caring Work." Radcliffe Public Policy Center, Cambridge, Mass., 1999.

Stone, D. Reframing Home Health-care Policy. Radcliffe Public Policy Center, Cambridge, Mass., 2000.

Stone, D. "Why We Need a Care Movement." *The Nation* 270, no. 10 (2000).

Sullivan, W. *Work and Integrity*. New York: Harper Business, 1995.

Thompson, E. P. "Time, Work-Discipline, and Industrial Capitalism." *Past and Present* 29 (1964): 61.

Tobias, R. "Global Transformations: Lessons for American Businesses." Radcliffe Public Policy Center, Cambridge, Mass., 1998.

Tocqueville, A. d. *Democracy in America*. New York: Doubleday, Anchor Books, 1969.

"Too Many Hours." *Boston Globe*. 7 April 2000.

U.S. Dept. of Commerce, Bureau of the Census. *Historical Statistics of the United States, Colonial Times to 1970*. White Plains, N.Y.: Kraus International Publications, 1989.

U.S. Kerner Commission. *Report of the National Advisory Commission on Civil Disorders*. New York: Bantam Books, 1968.

United Nations. Human Development Report. New York: United Nations Development Program, 1999.

Urban Institute National Survey of American Families. *Snapshots of American Families Health Insurance Coverage*. N. Brennan, J. Holahan and G. Kenny. Urban Institute, Washington, D.C., 1998.

Veblen, T. *The Theory of the Leisure Class*. New Brunswick, N.J.: Transaction Publishers, 1991.

Whitebook, M., and D. Bellm. *Taking on Turnover*. Washington, D.C.: Center for the Childcare Workforce, 1999.

Whitman, M. v. N. *New World, New Rules: The Changing Role of the American Corporation*. Cambridge: Harvard University Press, 1999.

Wilson, W. J. *When Work Disappears: The World of the New Urban Poor*. New York: Knopf, 1996.

Wuthnow, R. *Acts of Compassion: Caring for Others and Helping Ourselves*. Princeton: Princeton University Press, 1991.

Wuthnow, R. *Poor Richard's Principle: Recovering the American Dream Through the Moral Dimension of Work, Business, and Money*. Princeton, N.J.: Princeton University Press, 1996.

Wuthnow, R. *Loose Connections: Journey Together in America's Fragmental Communities*. Cambridge: Harvard University Press, 1998.

Yu, E. Y., ed. *Black-Korean Encounter: Toward Understanding and Alliance*. Los Angeles: Regina Books, 1994.

INDEX